Rails-to-Trails
Maryland, Delaware, Virginia, West Virginia

"There's no better guide for these multipurpose trails. Like the Rails-to-Trails system, this series is a service that's long overdue."

—Sarah Parsons, Associate Editor, *Sports Afield*

"Recreation trails are one of America's great outdoor secrets, but probably won't be for much longer thanks to the Rails-to-Trails Conservancy Guidebook Series. Now adventurers of all abilities have an excellent guide to help them enjoy all that the paths have to offer."

—Stephen Madden, Editor-in-Chief, *Outdoor Explorer*

"Kudos to Barbara Noe for providing such an invaluable guidebook to some of the country's best rail-trails. Her quick and easy-to-read details get us on the trail fast, while the historical mentions add spark. Now we're looking forward to the entire series."

—Linda Frahm, Managing Editor, *Walking Magazine*

"It's the attention to detail that makes each chapter and every trail come alive. . . . This kind of research and clear writing is seldom found in today's trail guides."

—Marc Sani, Editor-in-Chief, *Bike* magazine

Help Us Keep This Guide Up to Date

Every effort has been made by the author and editors to make this guide as accurate and useful as possible. However, many things can change after a guide is published—establishments close, phone numbers change, facilities come under new management, housing costs fluctuate, and so on.

We would love to hear from you concerning your experiences with this guide and how you feel it could be made better and be kept up to date. While we may not be able to respond to all comments and suggestions, we'll take them to heart and we'll make certain to share them with the author. Please send your comments and suggestions to the following address:

The Globe Pequot Press
Reader Response/Editorial Department
P.O. Box 480
Guilford, CT 06437

Or you may e-mail us at:

editorial@globe-pequot.com

Thanks for your input, and happy travels!

Great Rail-Trails Series

THE OFFICIAL

Rails-to-Trails

CONSERVANCY GUIDEBOOK

Maryland ▼ Delaware
Virginia ▼ West Virginia

by
Barbara A. Noe

The
Globe
Pequot
Press

Guilford, CT 06437

Cover illustration: Neal Aspinall
Cover design: Nancy Freeborn
Text design: Lesley Weissman-Cook
Maps: Tim Kissel/Trailhead Graphics, Inc.; © The Globe Pequot Press

Photo credits: Pp. xii, 34, 54, 55, 56, 70, 76, 77, 100, 102, 126, 134, 188, 193: photos by Keith Moore; p. 8: photo by Baltimore & Annapolis Trail Park Staff; p. 68: photo by Paul Durbin; pp. 90, 92, 93, 95: photos by Linda Richardson, Virginia Memories Photography; pp. 157, 160, 174, 175, 177: courtesy of West Virginia Division of Tourism & Parks, photos by Steve Shaluta, Jr.; p. 158: courtesy of West Virginia Division of Tourism & Parks, photo by Larry Belcher; all other photos by Barbara A. Noe.

Library of Congress Cataloging-in-Publication Data
Rails-to-trails : Maryland, Delaware, Virginia, West Virginia / Barbara
  A. Noe.—1st ed.
    p. cm. — (Great rail-trails series)
  ISBN 0-7627-0604-X
    1. Rail-trails—Maryland—Guidebooks. 2. Rail-trails—Delaware—Guide-
books. 3. Rail-trails—Virginia—Guidebooks. 4. Rail-trails—West Virginia—
Guidebooks. 5. Outdoor recreation—Maryland—Guidebooks. 6. Outdoor
recreation—Delaware—Guidebooks. 7. Outdoor recreation—Virginia—
Guidebooks. 8. Outdoor recreation—West Virginia—Guidebooks. I. Noe,
Barbara A. II. Series.

GV191.42.M3 R35 2000
917.504'43—dc21   99-057289

Manufactured in the United States of America
First Edition/Fourth Printing

This book is dedicated with love to my parents.

CONTENTS

WEST VIRGINIA

West Virginia's Top Rail-Trails

More Rail-Trails

ACKNOWLEDGMENTS

This book is a finished product thanks to the concerted effort of many people. All of the trail managers were overwhelmingly helpful in providing information and checking each piece for accuracy. Thanks especially to Allen Barker, Travis Campbell, David Dionne, Kyle Gulbronson, Katy Miller, Joe Powers, and Ralph Young. Hugh Morris and Mark Hurley of the Rails-to-Trails Conservancy kindly allowed me complete access to the Conservancy's prolific research files. Frank Proud of the West Virginia Rails-to-Trails Council shared tons of research material for the West Virginia trails, and was invaluable in the trail selection process.

Special thanks goes to Keith Moore, who accompanied me on many of the trails, and diligently researched much of the text. He also wrote the Cranberry/Tri-Rivers Rail-Trail. Sean M. Groom wrote the North Bend Rail-Trail. And merci beaucoup to my other trail companions, as well as those who had to put up with me during the frantic deadline days: Kim Cartwright, Saundra Crane, Paul Durbin, Monica Ekman, and Leslie Ricketts.

· INTRODUCTION

On a bright spring day, there's no better place to be than atop Virginia's Whitetop Mountain, with nowhere to go but down. And so you follow the forested Virginia Creeper Trail deep into a highland landscape of rippling, blue-gray ridges and new-green pastures, deep gullies and boulder-tossed streams. Redbuds and dogwoods add splashes of bright pink and snow white to the remote green woodlands, and seventy-five wooden trestles beckon you to their railings, where you can scan the pellucid green waters below for flashes of fish. Hungry? Stop in Damascus for pizza or a sandwich or picnic supplies. Tired? Stay overnight at one of Abingdon's B&Bs. What a great life.

And this is just one sampling of the rail-trails that this guidebook has to offer. There's Virginia's Cape Henry Trail and its bald cypress swamp; the intimate paths of West Virginia's Tea Creek Recreation Area, ideal for backpacking and mountain biking; the Capital Crescent Trail, a popular commuter route that whisks Washingtonians through a tunnel of bird-filled trees between Washington and Maryland. And many, many more, embracing a melee of plush pastureland, genteel riverscapes, skyscraping mountain peaks, and leafy neighborhoods.

There is no strict definition of a rail-trail. Often they are long, skinny parks (many just a couple of yards wide) in the middle of a city, buffeted from housing developments and strip malls by only a thin row of trees. The region is graced with many of these: the Capital Crescent Trail; The Washington & Old Dominion Railroad Trail (W&OD), which transports Washingtonians to the lush Virginia piedmont; the Greater Wheeling Trail, which slithers along the mighty Ohio River through the heart of downtown Wheeling, West Virginia. These corridors provide urban dwellers with a woodsy, virtually level trail that is ideal for

The epitome of Virginia Highlands beauty is on view at Taylors Valley along the Virginia Creeper Trail.

hiking, biking, in-line skating—and commuting—all in their own back-yards. And, just as humans flock to these natural bastions, so do birds, white-tailed deer, and clouds of butterflies. Bring your binoculars.

A whole other category of rail-trails is the rural rail-trail—the likes of the Virginia Creeper; the New River Trail, which hugs the New River in Virginia for 57 miles as it wanders through cow-speckled pastures; and the rustic Northern Central Rail Trail in Maryland, just north of Baltimore. Oftentimes these trails pass through old boom towns, many of which are finding new life with the B&Bs, bike shops, and little restaurants that are popping up to serve the trail users—an instant boost to local economies. And a definite reason to make a day or weekend of it.

And then there are the mountain trails of West Virginia—sinewy paths that wander up and around rugged peaks, opening up some of the most stupendous scenery around. The Limerock Trail, for instance, creeps down the remote face of Blackwater Canyon; the Gauley Mountain Trail explores the spruce-dotted realm of the Tea Creek Recreation Area, in the heart of black bear country. These offer no facilities; it's just you and nature.

Maryland, Delaware, Virginia, and West Virginia are truly blessed with a diversity of rail-trails. But, as different as the trails are from one another, they all share a common theme: They are all legacies of the vast railroad network that defined the landscape beginning in the early 1800s. In fact, the nation's first steam locomotive made its first run from Baltimore to Ellicott Mills (now Ellicott City) in 1813. Railroads played a strategic role in the Civil War, transporting troops and supplies to the front line and carrying wounded soldiers back. Later, railroads opened up the remote wilderness of southern Virginia and West Virginia, as their tracks laced mountains to access coal, oil, and timber.

Americorps contributed much to the fruition of the Harrison County Parks and Recreation Bike & Hike Trail.

The trails' main focus now is recreation. But if you look care-

The C&O Canal begins in Lower Georgetown.

fully you'll find souvenirs of the past—keep your eyes peeled for cookie-cutter depots, old whistle-stops, exchange boxes, crosses and ties, and random spikes. And sometimes, when the breeze moves just right, you may confuse the roar of an accompanying stream for the clamor of an oncoming train . . . .

The Rail-Trail Movement

The rail-trails included in this book are part of a nationwide movement to convert rails to multiuse trails. In the early 1900s, the United States boasted the world's most extensive network of railroads tracks, connecting virtually every community—those towns that the railroad bypassed basically withered and blew away. At the peak of the railroad's golden age, in 1916, more than 300,000 miles of track crisscrossed the country. But bit by bit, automobiles, buses, trucks, and planes upstaged the railroad; now 3,000 miles of track are abandoned every year.

The idea to use these old rail beds as ready-made trails began in the Midwest, where railroad abandonments were most widespread. Locals walked or hiked these fairly level, tree-shaded corridors, keeping an eye out for old railroading relics. While popular informally, it was another story to actually motivate an official movement to preserve these rails as trails. From the early 1960s to the 1980s, trail proponents fought an uphill battle against developers, who were able to outbid them for land.

Then in 1983, Congress passed the National Trails System Act, which directed the Surface Transportation Board to set aside for future rail use any rights-of-way about to be abandoned (called railbanking), while permitting them to be used as trails in the interim. Trail organizers and local proponents had a better chance to acquire the rights of way—although short deadlines, lack of information dissemination, and local opposition to trails still created problems.

In 1986 the Rails-to-Trails Conservancy was formed to support the national expansion of rails to trails. The Conservancy dedicated itself to preserving rail corridors, developing a national advocacy law to defend the railbanking law, and assisting public agencies and local groups in rail-trail conversion. At the start, the Rails-to-Trails Conservancy knew of only thirty-five rail-trails in the entire country, with ninety in the works. Today, that number tops 1,000, comprising more than 10,000 miles of public trails that, in 1999, were used 100 million times by bikers, hikers, bird-watchers, campers, anglers, in-line skaters, horseback riders, and all other kinds of outdoor enthusiasts. In addition, more than 1,200 other projects are underway. The ultimate goal of creating an interconnected network of trails across the country—just as the railroads once did—is rapidly being realized.

How to Use This Guide

The major rail-trails in this book were selected for their recreational potential, ease of access, high use, aesthetic appeal, and special interest for natural or cultural history. Arranged alphabetically by state, they are treated with mile-by-mile descriptions. The region's other rail-trails are listed alphabetically, at the end of each state chapter, with shorter summary descriptions.

Remember that rail-trails are works in progress. As such, it's always wise to call the trail contacts ahead of time for the most up-to-date information. Likewise, natural disasters such as flooding and rock slides can close trails, make them difficult to access, or make surfaces tough to negotiate. One phone call can save a lot of hassle.

All information has been checked and is accurate to the best of the author's knowledge as of press time. If you find that changes have been made to the trails, or that an establishment has gone out of business, please let us know so that we may correct future editions.

Hop aboard and enjoy!

Key to Activities Icons

 Backpacking

 Bird-watching

 Camping

 Cross-country Skiing

 Fishing

 Historic Sites

 Horseback Riding

 In-line Skating

 Mountain Biking

 Paddlesports

 Road Bicycling

 Running

 Swimming

 Walking/Dayhiking

 Wildlife Viewing

Key to Map Icons

 Parking

 Information

Restrooms

 Rentals

Camping

MARYLAND AND DELAWARE

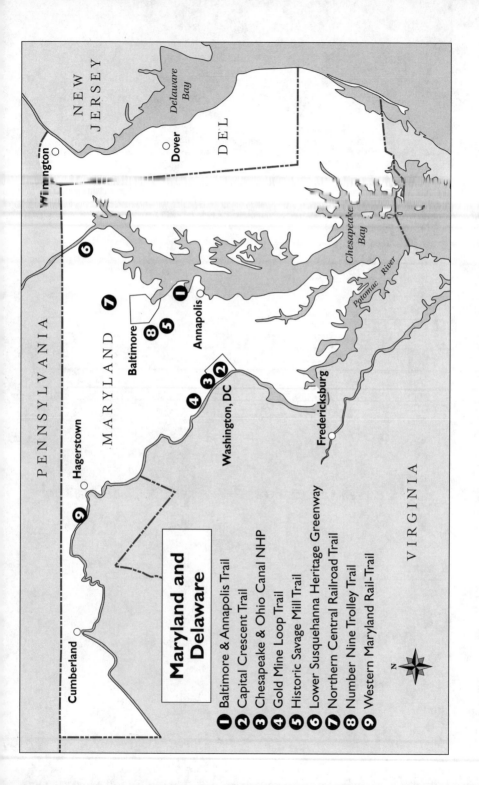

Maryland and Delaware

1. Baltimore & Annapolis Trail
2. Capital Crescent Trail
3. Chesapeake & Ohio Canal NHP
4. Gold Mine Loop Trail
5. Historic Savage Mill Trail
6. Lower Susquehanna Heritage Greenway
7. Northern Central Railroad Trail
8. Number Nine Trolley Trail
9. Western Maryland Rail-Trail

INTRODUCTION

America's railroading age was born in Maryland in 1830, when the B&O's *Tom Thumb* left Baltimore for Ellicott City in stiff competition with a horse-drawn carriage. Carrying forty passengers and chugging along at a respectable 10 miles an hour, the diminutive steam engine lost to the horses, but nevertheless proved to naysayers that steam traction was feasible on steep, winding grades. Back then, no one envisioned how successful the newfangled railroad would be, how its great network of rails would come to lace the entire country, carrying goods and passengers back and forth. And no one foresaw how, a century down the line, retired tracks would be converted into a fantastic network of recreational rail-trails.

As history would dictate, Maryland has a number of excellent rail-trails, among them the rural Northern Central Railroad Trail in the northern part of the state, noted for carrying President Abraham Lincoln to deliver his Gettysburg address, and the Baltimore & Annapolis Trail south of Baltimore, a glorious woodsy escape in the heart of one of Maryland's most populous counties. Joining these are the Lower Susquehanna Heritage Greenway, a portion of an enormous project underway that showcases the Susquehanna River and its bald eagles, and the Historic Savage Mill Trail, a short jaunt along an especially pretty section of the Little Patuxent River. Among the newest trails is the Western Maryland Rail Trail, a fast, paved path in the Appalachian foothills just west of Hagerstown.

Closely intertwined with the story of the railroad is that of the canal—ancient Roman technology made obsolete only by the arrival of the iron horse. Their towpaths, too, make ideal trails for walking, hiking, biking, and horseback riding. Maryland boasts the nation's best-preserved canal system, the Chesapeake & Ohio Canal, with an enchanting towpath that follows the Potomac River for 184.5 miles between Washington, D.C., and Cumberland, Maryland.

And let's not forget the train's smaller sibling, the electric trolley. Maryland has converted several old trolley routes into trails, including the woodsy Number Nine Trolley Trail in Ellicott City and the Gold Mine Loop Trail at Great Falls.

(continued)

Topping off this smorgasbord of converted transportation tracks are many more in the works. Funding was recently acquired for the North Bethesda Trail (formerly called the Bethesda Trolley Trail); the Chesapeake Loop Trail is being worked on; and there are many more to look forward to.

Delaware, too, has plenty of railroading history. The New Castle and Frenchtown Railroad was its first, providing the rail link in the water-rail-water route from Philadelphia to Baltimore beginning in 1831 (with horse-drawn cars!). The first railroad merger in the United States was between the Wilmington and Susquehanna Railroad and the Delaware and Maryland Railroad in 1836. Despite this breadth of history, however, the rail-trail movement has been slow in coming to Delaware. For now, two trails are partially open, with a trail connecting Lewes and Rehoboth Beach in the works. (For information on the Delaware trails, see "More Rail-Trails" toward the end of this section of the book.)

Maryland's

TOP RAIL-TRAILS

1 Baltimore & Annapolis Trail Park

Edged with tulip poplars, pocket wetlands, and conventions of wildflowers, this easy trail gently winds through mostly wooded surroundings—a world away from the area's impossible congestion.

Activities:

Location: From Annapolis to Glen Burnie, in Anne Arundel County, Maryland

Length: 13.3 miles one-way

Surface: Asphalt

Wheelchair access: Yes. The paved, flat trail is ideal for wheelchairs; the Earleigh Heights Ranger Station has a wheelchair-accessible rest room and a wheelchair fitness course.

Difficulty: Easy. The trail is straight and flat—perfect for young riders—but, there are many road crossings where bikers must dismount.

Food: The trail runs parallel to MD–2, which features a spectrum of eating establishments. Among the many choices are the restaurants and fast-food joints at Arnold Station (mile 1), Severna Park (mile 5), Jumpers Hole (mile 9), and Marley Station (mile 10.5).

Rest rooms: Earleigh Heights Ranger Station (mile 7), Marley Station Mall (mile 10.5).

Seasons: Open year-round. Wildflowers line the trailside in spring and summer.

Access and parking: Access and parking are available at the end points of the trail and at many points along the way:

- *Boulters Way:* The Anne Arundel County of Recreation and Parks, which maintains the trail, offers two parking lots. One is at the southern terminus on Boulters Way; from U.S. 50 just east of Annapolis, follow MD–450 south of exit 27 toward the Naval Academy to Boulters Way.

- *Earleigh Heights Ranger Station:* The other is in the middle of the trail at the Earleigh Heights Ranger Station (mile 7), on Earleigh Heights Road, just off MD–2.
- *Marley Station Mall:* Shopping centers and side roads along the way offer countless access and parking possibilities; the most popular is Marley Station Mall, at mile 10.5, near the junction of MD–100 and MD–2.

Rentals: There are a few bike rental shops nearby.

- Pedal Pushers Bike Shop, 546 Baltimore Annapolis Boulevard, Severna Park, MD 21146; (410) 544–2323.
- Bike Peddlers, 5 Central Avenue, Glen Burnie, MD 21061; (410) 761–7675.

Contact: Superintendent, Baltimore & Annapolis Trail Park, P.O. Box 1007, Severna Park, MD 21146-8007; (410) 222–6244.

• •

Wedged between strip malls and housing developments near car-choked MD–2, this breath of fresh air embraces riots of blooming wildflowers, plush green horse farms, tulip trees, and stone-dotted creeks. Your route is the Baltimore & Annapolis Trail, built along the former rail bed of the B&A Short Line Railroad. Granted, it doesn't have the remote feel of, say, the Northern Central Railroad Trail farther north, but considering nearly 50 percent of all of Anne Arundel County's residents live within a mile of the trail, the B&A is a precious gem indeed. Locals use it to go shopping and to school, as well as a convenient nature escape. As such, the trail is nearly always busy, excessively so on pleasant weekends. But an early morning stroll can still stir up a white-tailed deer and her fawn, or a red-headed woodpecker tapping on a fallen log.

One of the nicest things about this trail is the abundance of wildflowers that flourish in spring and summer—many planted along the split-rail fences and tended by community groups. Japanese honeysuckle blooms perfume the air from April through September; white and yellow daisies bob in the breeze between May and August, especially between the MD–100 bridge and the Round Bay Bridge; and sweet Queen Anne's lace thrives between May and October. Also sprinkling the trailside are old ties, restored train stations, and switch boxes, reminders of the route's railroading days.

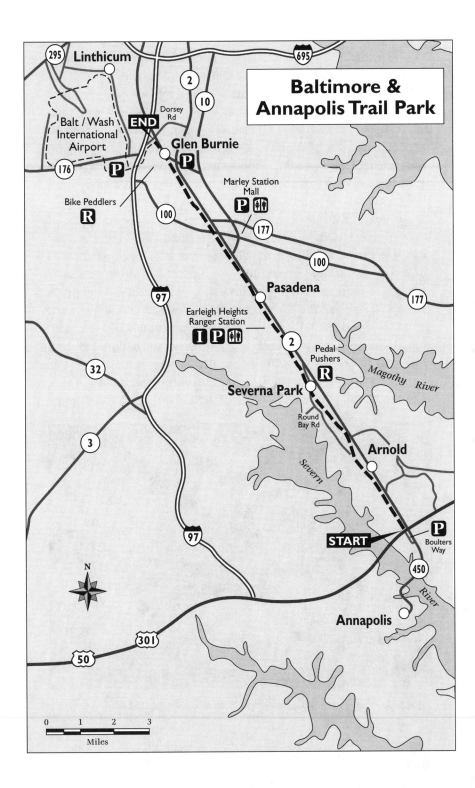

Baltimore & Annapolis Trail Park

295 Linthicum

695

2

10

Dorsey Rd

END Glen Burnie

Balt / Wash International Airport

176 P

Bike Peddlers R

Marley Station Mall P 🚻

177

100

100

97

Pasadena

Earleigh Heights Ranger Station I P 🚻

2

Pedal Pushers R

Magothy River

32

Severna Park

Round Bay Rd

Severn

Arnold

3

97

START

P Boulters Way

450

N

River

Annapolis

301

50

0 1 2 3
Miles

The Baltimore & Annapolis Short Line Railroad carried passengers and freight between Maryland's capital and its largest city from 1887 to 1968. At first trains traveled through undeveloped countryside, a backwater of fields and woods dotted with country stores, churches, and schools, but no towns. All that soon changed, when the government authorized six post offices along the route and some towns flourished (though others failed), a canning industry thrived near the tracks, and people moved to the countryside, where they could enjoy rural living with the convenience of big-city amenities within reach.

Around the turn of the century, steam engines were replaced by sleek electric cars, complete with stained-glass windows and mahogany trim. As nice as they looked, the train couldn't shed its nicknames: "Bumble & Amble," "Bounce & Agitate," "Bumps & Agony," to name a few. Regardless, as one journalist wrote, passengers "cherished the B&A as one might a decrepit and awkward but faithful body servant." Passenger service stopped in 1952, with freight service continuing until 1968. As part of the national rails-to-trails movement, the B&A Trail officially opened in 1990.

It's no secret that the southern portion of the trail is more scenic than the north, where shopping malls and housing developments

In-line skaters and bikers share the woodsy Baltimore & Annapolis Trail.

encroach. As such, this jaunt begins from the southern terminus; you can go all the way to Glen Burnie if you'd like, but most people turn around midway at the ranger station. Leaving the Boulters Way parking area, follow Boulters Way to the trailhead, about a half a mile away, and turn right, onto the trail. Before you lies the tree-fringed path, alive with birdsong and showcasing stately tulip poplars. You cross several streets, and houses remind you that you are indeed in suburbia—but these houses are large and beautiful, with plenty of trees and lawn. Now and again you cross a creek surrounded by pockets of tangled, verdant undergrowth.

At mile 3.4 is Jones Station Road, with drinking water, a phone, a shade shelter, and benches. A bit farther along, between mile 4 and Round Bay Road, you can see the remains of a spur that once led to Round Bay, a turn-of-the-century summer resort. Baltimoreans would take excursion trains to enjoy the beach, staying at the grand "Hotel," and dancing at a large pavilion.

The trail takes on a more suburban feel as you enter the town of Severna Park (mile 4.8), a nineteenth-century farming community owned by the Linstead family. You parallel Baltimore Annapolis Boulevard a bit, crossing two fairly busy streets. Be careful! Pavilions and benches provide a chance to stop and rest. At Riggs Avenue stands the Severna Park station, a brick building surrounded by a white picket fence. Home to the Severna Park Model Railroad Club since 1969, it's the only brick station along the entire line.

The trail continues through pretty woodlands filled with oaks, maples, and grapevines. Keep your eyes open for cottontails nibbling the clover-dotted grass, bright red cardinals darting among the branches, fields of white and yellow daisies in early June. Packtown (mile 6.2) is an old settlement of freed slaves dating from before the Civil War. James Pack and his family, according to the census, lived here as early as 1830. More freed slaves joined them over the following years; most of today's residents have inherited their land. The close-knit neighborhood, with its large gardens and twisty roads, has so far evaded development.

At mile 7 you come to the Earleigh Heights Ranger Station— marking the trail's unofficial halfway point. The glorious Victorian-era structure once served as a post office (originally named Frost's), general store, and train station. Drinking water, picnic tables, rest rooms, telephone, and parking for forty vehicles are all available here, with some small historical exhibits inside. On the trail's east side, next to old Listman's general store (still open for refreshments), stands a prime example of a Sears Roebuck catalog home, ordered by mail about 1924, delivered by railroad, and assembled on the spot. The next house over has several railroad artifacts in the backyard, including signals and a switch box.

Leaving the ranger station, you pass a mix of new and old homes, intermingled with commercial development. At mile 10.5, skirt the Marley Station Mall, named for the station that once stood on the site of present-day Hecht's. Soon you cross over Marley Creek, the largest creek on the trail. The original 140-foot railroad bridge here was washed out by Hurricane Agnes in 1972. At the time the B&A Trail was being planned, the county acquired an 1875 highway bridge from Polk County, Missouri, to take its place. In 1989, as workers put the bridge together, improper lifting caused it to collapse into a pile of scrap. Whoops! So the construction company responsibly built the similar structure that you see today.

Onward, the trail is fairly perfunctory, squeezed between rows of suburban houses. Harundale Mall (mile 11.8) is the first closed mall east of the Mississippi River. You proceed through residential areas into the city of Glen Burnie. Before the coming of the trail, the old railroad corridor here was an open-air drug market, and opponents thought that the rail-trail would facilitate crime and vandalism. Nothing could have been further from the truth. The community rallied with trail staff to drive it all out, so that the trail is lovely, impeccably maintained.

The B&A ends at Dorsey Road (mile 13.3), where it connects with the nearly complete Baltimore & Washington International Airport Trail, a 14.5-mile paved loop around the airport offering superb landing and take-off views; contact the Anne Arundel County Department of Recreation and Parks at (410) 222–6244 for information.

2 Capital Crescent Trail/ Georgetown Branch Interim Trail

Named for the crescent-shaped path it takes through the District and Montgomery County, this tree-lined trail transports commuters and outdoor enthusiasts through quiet, wooded neighborhoods and parklands, along the banks of the Potomac River and beyond.

Activities:

Notes: Road bikes are fine for the first 7 miles; mountain bikes or hybrids are recommended for last 4 miles of gravel

Location: From Georgetown in Washington, D.C., to Silver Spring, Maryland

Length: 11 miles one-way

Surface: Asphalt and crushed gravel (Georgetown Branch extension)

Wheelchair access: Yes. The first 7 miles include a bit of an uphill, but the path is paved and smooth. The crushed gravel trail beyond Bethesda is also suitable for wheelchairs.

Difficulty: Moderate. The section between Fletcher's Boathouse and River Road has a pretty good, gradual climb; the paved surface makes it quick for bikes.

Food: Restaurants and sandwich shops in Georgetown (near the trailhead); Fletcher's Boathouse (mile 8) has a snack bar; groceries and restaurants in Bethesda (mile 3.5).

Rest rooms: Fletcher's Boathouse (mile 8) is your best bet.

Seasons: Open year-round. Spring and fall are both lovely, with colorful foliage and migrant birds, while in summer the dense shade of mature trees makes the trail a cool respite. Winter can be windy and chilly.

Access and parking: Public parking and access can be found in several locations:
- *At the trailhead:* This is on the west end of K Street (called Water Street), near the Key Bridge in lower Georgetown.
- *Fletcher's Boathouse* (mile 8): Located at 4940 Canal Road, N.W., north of Georgetown.
- *Bethesda* (mile 3.5): around Bethesda Avenue.
- Access is also available on any number of cross streets (consult the map).

Rentals: Boat and bike rentals are available along the way:

- Thompson Boat Center, 2900 Virginia Avenue, N.W., Washington, D.C. 20037; (202) 333–9543; located near the trailhead at the intersection of Rock Creek Parkway and Virginia Avenue in Georgetown; rents bikes April–October.
- Fletcher's Boathouse (mile 8), 4940 Canal Road, N.W., Washington, D.C. 20007; (202) 244–0461; also rents bikes April–October.
- Griffin Cycle, Inc., 4949 Bethesda Avenue, Bethesda, MD 20814; (301) 656–6188; rents bikes year round.

Contact. For the latest information on trail conditions call the recording at (202) 234–4874. The managing agency for the D.C. section is C&O Canal National Historical Park, P.O. Box 4, Sharpsburg, MD 21782; (301) 739–4200. The managing agency for the Maryland section is the Maryland–National Capital Park and Planning Commission, Montgomery County Parks, 9500 Brunett Avenue, Silver Spring, MD 20901; (301) 495–2466. Also, write the Coalition for the Capital Crescent Trail, P.O. Box 30703, Bethesda, MD 20824.

• • • • • • • • • • • • • • • • • • •

A woodsy corridor through some of the Washington area's most crowded neighborhoods, the Capital Crescent Trail (CCT) rates not only as an extremely popular commuter bike route, but also as a favorite weekend destination. There's a rare moment that you actually have the trail to yourself, but with 100 avian species, 92 varieties of trees and shrubs, and 160 types of wildflowers, ranging from Adder's tongue to yarrow, this trail is a nature lover's delight. Beginning in Georgetown, it climbs a gentle grade to Bethesda, where it connects with a temporary 4-mile gravel extension to Silver Spring.

The CCT lies along the abandoned Georgetown Spur, which, between 1910 and 1985, ran 11 miles between the Baltimore & Ohio Railroad in Silver Spring to Georgetown. Lumbering freight trains hauled construction supplies and fuel, but no passengers. After the train stopped running in 1984, the dream for the recreational trail began. Originally destined to be a narrow, disjointed path, it mushroomed into what you see today: a marvelous trail that cost millions of dollars to build—and it's not done yet. There's controversy brewing over whether to build a trolley line along the rail-trail between the downtowns of Bethesda and Silver Spring (that's why this segment is surfaced in inexpensive gravel), and there are grandiose plans of linking the loop to Union Station, along the proposed Metropolitan Branch

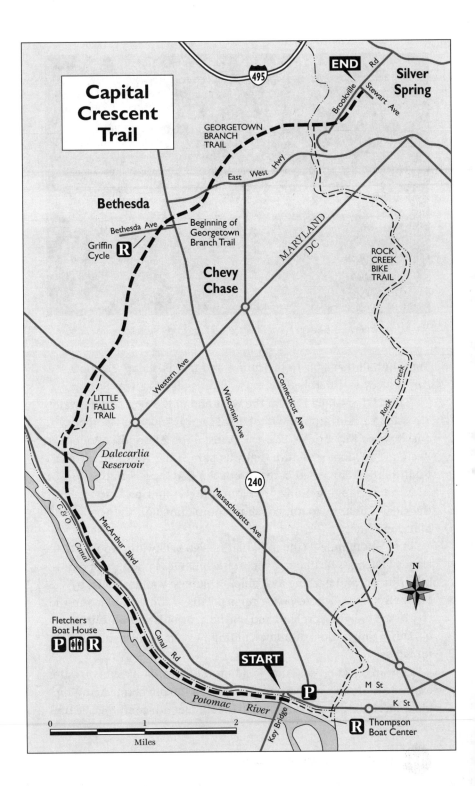

The hidden Little Falls Bike and Foot Trail is just off the Capital Crescent Trail at mile 6.

Trail. But all that's far in the future and talk is cheap. For now, we can be very satisfied with a pretty jaunt as far as Silver Spring.

The CCT trailhead lies at the west end of K Street (called Water Street here), beneath the Whitehurst Freeway in lower Georgetown. Just beyond Key Bridge, pass the ruins of the Alexandria Aqueduct Arch, a 1,100-foot structure that was part of the Alexandria Canal. Built in 1843, it carried barges from the C&O Canal to the port of Alexandria. Moving along, you join the glimmering Potomac and the C&O Canal towpath, constant companions all the way to the Maryland line.

Just before mile 8 (the mile markers go backward, from 11 to 0) stands Fletcher's Boathouse, with refreshments, a phone, rest rooms, bike rentals, and parking available. Be sure to wander down by the Potomac's edge, where peace reigns. This is the best place in the city to see breeding orchard and northern orioles and warbling vireos. During migration, swallows, chimney swifts, gulls, and Caspian terns pass by.

Onward, you cross Canal Road on the Arizona Avenue Trestle; examine its double spans, fine examples of the pin-connected Whipple trapezoidal design perfected in the nineteenth century. The trail moves up the Potomac bluffs, and finally at the Maryland line you leave the river and towpath for good. You soon enter the dark chasm of the Dalecarlia Tunnel, its portals draped with twisted foliage. Completed in 1910, the redbrick tunnel took the rail spur (and now you!) under MacArthur Boulevard. Trees envelop the trail farther along, which takes on a remote feel despite the fact that you know houses aren't too far away.

You roam through leafy Little Falls Park, filled with birdsong in spring. For something different, try taking the more intimate Little Falls Bike and Foot Trail beside riffling Little Falls Run (at mile 6 take the paved trail to the right, toward the reservoir), a dog-walking paradise. Otherwise, keep going through the woods, crossing over Massachusetts Avenue (just before mile marker 5). Beyond, you come to the former site of the Loughborough Mill, built in the early 1800s by Nathan Loughborough and used to grind flour for the Georgetown wheat trade. It operated until the Civil War, when the family fled south to serve the Confederacy.

The trailscape becomes decidedly more suburban as you proceed across River Road (mile 4.5), Little Falls Parkway (just after mile 4),

and Bradley Boulevard (just before mile 3.5), straight into the heart of Bethesda. At Bethesda Avenue (beyond mile 3.5), watch for the green and white signs leading you to the newly completed Wisconsin Avenue Tunnel, which whisks you beneath busy Wisconsin Avenue to the Georgetown Branch Interim Trail.

The Georgetown Branch Interim Trail—a smooth, hardpacked gravel path—connects the CCT with Silver Spring, 4 miles away. Ever following the route of former steam engines, the rustic trail passes East-West

Two bikers exit the historic Dalecarlia Tunnel on the Capital Crescent Trail.

Highway and ambles through the emerald greens of Columbia Country Club and tony neighborhoods. The one missing link is where the CCT crosses over Rock Creek Park: The original trestle was damaged as a result of arson a few years back, and so you must take an alternate route. The well-marked detour begins at the corner of Jones Mill and Jones Bridge Roads. After crossing the intersection, follow Susanna Lane down to the Rock Creek Bike Trail. This trail jogs through the park, across Rock Creek, and beneath the seriously dilapidated trestle. From here, signs lead you back to the Georgetown Branch trail via Freyman Drive and Grubb Road. The trail ends unceremoniously less than a mile beyond the detour, just beyond Stewart Avenue.

I would seriously recommend forgetting this last mile of the trail, which is a tad overgrown and unimpressive. Instead, consider staying on the Rock Creek Bike Trail and returning to Georgetown via Rock Creek Park, D.C.'s largest block of forest. At the District line, you can hop onto Beach Drive, which is closed to traffic on weekends. A couple of sites may tempt you to stop for a rest: Pierce Mill, a nineteenth-century gristmill that's now a museum; and the National Zoo, home to a giant panda, Komodo dragons, and rare Sumatran tigers.

Nearing Georgetown, cross Pennsylvania Avenue, M Street, and K Street. When you reach Thompson Boat Center, cut through down to the river, turn right along the brick path, and enjoy the Potomac views as you make your way back to Water Street.

3 Chesapeake & Ohio Canal National Historical Park

The Chesapeake & Ohio Canal was built between 1828 and 1850 with the intention of linking Chesapeake Bay ports with the Ohio Valley. Rendered obsolete by the railroad even before it was completed, the canal became a national historical park in 1971, its towpath offering a serene pathway along the Potomac. Moving from tidewater at Rock Creek in Georgetown to the mountain town of Cumberland, deep in the Appalachians, the trail gets wilder the farther west you go, finally entering a landscape that still belongs to the ducks and white-tailed deer, foxes and great blue herons.

Activities:

Notes: There are free hiker/biker campsites every 5 miles between miles 16 and 180. Drive-in camping areas are located at McCoys Ferry, Fifteen Mile Creek, and Spring Gap. Each campsite has a water pump (May–November), portable toilet, picnic table, and fire hole. First come, first served. Major stops are conveniently located along the trail about 30 miles apart, perfect for planning overnights in hotels or B&Bs. Horseback riding is not permitted between Georgetown and Swains Lock. Swimming is allowed in the Potomac, except from Chain Bridge to Great Falls.

Location: From Georgetown in Washington, D.C., to Cumberland, Maryland, along the Potomac River

Length: 184.5 miles one-way

Surface: Clay and crushed stone

Wheelchair access: There is a handicapped accessible walkway from the towpath to the Great Falls Overlook at Great Falls (mile 14.3).

Difficulty: Moderate. The conditions vary from excellent to rough, due to tree roots, potholes, rocks, and weather conditions. Periodic floods can wreak havoc on sections of the canal, which take time to repair. It's best to phone ahead. The busiest section of the towpath is from Washington to Seneca (miles 1–23) and near Harpers Ferry (mile 60.7); the most isolated sections

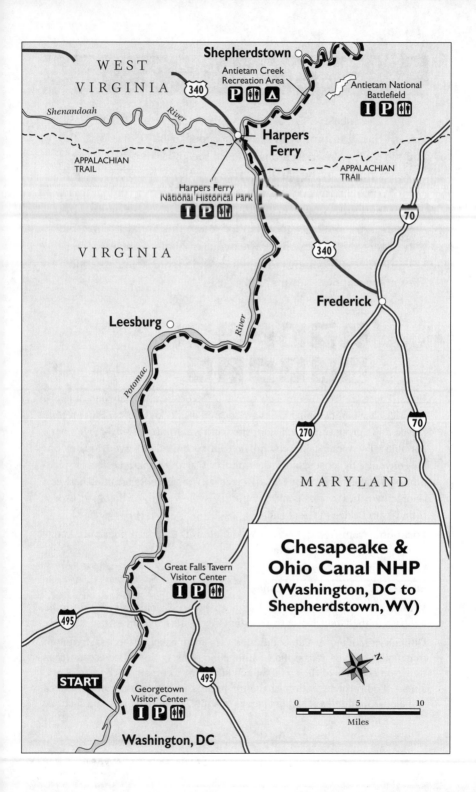

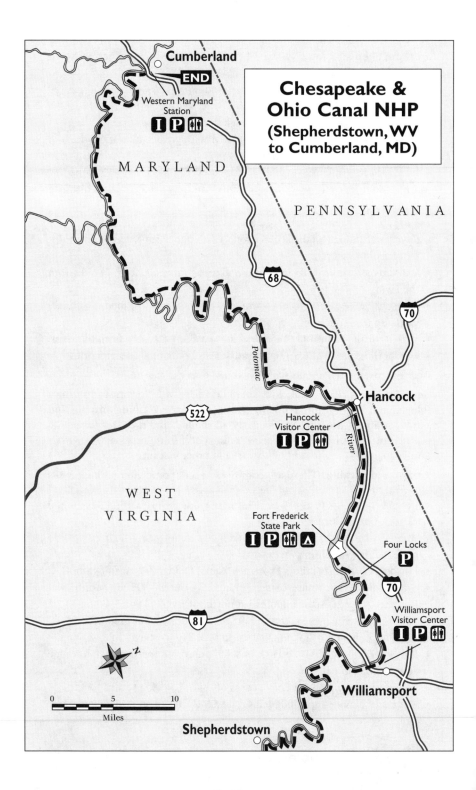

Cumberland

END

Western Maryland
Station
🛈 🅿 🚻

MARYLAND

PENNSYLVANIA

**Chesapeake &
Ohio Canal NHP**
(Shepherdstown, WV
to Cumberland, MD)

68

70

Potomac

Hancock

522

Hancock
Visitor Center
🛈 🅿 🚻

River

WEST
VIRGINIA

Fort Frederick
State Park
🛈 🅿 🚻 ⛺

Four Locks
🅿

70

Williamsport
Visitor Center
🛈 🅿 🚻

81

N

Williamsport

0   5   10
▬▬▬▬▬▬▬▬▬▬
Miles

Shepherdstown

are from Shepherdstown to Dam 4 (miles 70–85) and Hancock to North Branch (miles 125–180).

Food: Food stops are located about every 30 miles; it's always wise to carry snacks and water. Suggested stops:

- Fletcher's Boathouse (mile 3.1), snack bar.
- Great Falls Tavern (mile 14.3), snack bar with great pink lemonade.
- Swains Lock (mile 16.6), snack bar.
- Whites Ferry (mile 35.5), general store down by the river, with deli.
- Point of Rocks (mile 48.2), several stores on Clay Street, a short distance from river.
- Harpers Ferry (mile 60.7), restaurants and groceries.
- Snyders Landing (mile 76.6), Barron's C&O Canal Trail Store, a short distance from the river.
- Williamsport (mile 99.8), groceries and restaurants about a half mile from the river.
- Hancock (mile 124), grocery store, restaurants, and fast food, about 200 yards up from the river.
- Little Orleans (mile 140.9), general store a short distance from the river.
- Cumberland (mile 184.5), restaurants, fast-food joints, and groceries.

Rest rooms: Portable toilets are located at every campsite.

Seasons: Open year-round, with splendid spring wildflowers and autumn foliage, and migrant birds passing through. During Washington's hot and humid summer, the towpath is nearly all shaded, and the river keeps the temperature 10 to 15 degrees cooler; afternoon thunderstorms, however, are frequent. Winter is cold, with variable precipitation.

Access and parking: There are countless access points and parking areas along the length of the canal, variously accessible from Washington, D.C., via I–495, I–270, I–70, and I–68. The major ones, most with a designated parking lot, include:

- *Water Street/P Street in Georgetown* (mile 0): Short-term parking available underneath Whitehurst Freeway.
- *Fletcher's Boathouse* (mile 3.1): At 4940 Canal Road, N.W., Washington, D.C.
- *Great Falls Tavern Visitor Center* (mile 14.3): Take I–495 to Clara Barton Parkway and MacArthur Boulevard north.
- *Whites Ferry* (mile 35.5): Located off I–270 southwest of Frederick.
- *Brunswick* (mile 55): Take I–70 west to MD–340 west exit, follow signs.
- *Harpers Ferry* (mile 60.7): Park in town and cross the pedestrian bridge across the Potomac to towpath.
- *Williamsport* (mile 99.3): Easy access off I–81.
- *Fort Frederick State Park* (mile 112.4): Take MD–56 exit off I–70, follow signs.

The C&O Canal begins in Lower Georgetown.

- *Hancock Visitor Center* (mile 124): From I–70, follow MD–144 about a mile to downtown Hancock and follow signs.
- *Paw Paw, West Virginia* (mile 156.8): From I–70 follow U.S. 522 and WV–9 to parking area just beyond the town.
- *Cumberland Visitor Center* (mile 184.5): Take exit 43-C off I–68; at the bottom of the ramp make a left onto Harrison Street. The parking lot of TCI Cable and the Western Maryland Station Center is located at the end of the street. The canal towpath begins directly to the left of the station, almost directly under the I–68 bridge.

Rentals: There are several rentals nearby:

- Thompson Boat Center, 2900 Virginia Avenue, N.W., Washington, D.C. 20037; (202) 333–9543; April–October.
- Fletcher's Boathouse (mile 3.1), 4940 Canal Road, N.W., Washington, D.C. 20007; (202) 244–0461; April–October.
- Swains Lock (mile 16, north of Great Falls off River Road, on Swains Lock Road), 10700 Swains Lock, Potomac, MD 20854; (301) 299–9006; mid-March–mid-November.

Shuttle service: For those wanting to ride the entire length of the canal, from Cumberland to D.C., there's a private shuttle service that will take you and five friends to Cumberland (or pick you up there) for $45 each. Call

(800) TOUR–CNO for information. You could also rent a one-way U-Haul or Ryder truck for about $150 (great for a small group).

Contact: C&O Canal National Historical Park Headquarters, Box 4, Sharpsburg, MD 21782; (301) 739–4200.

• • • • • • • • • • • • • • • • • • • •

A green-shaded path winding beside the Potomac River from Washington, D.C., to Cumberland, Maryland, the Chesapeake & Ohio Canal is one of the nation's undiscovered treasures. Bluebell dotted banks, oak-covered mountains, stream-crossed woods, and thousands of springtime warblers are some of its delights, intermingled with hundreds of relics describing its past: old locks, whitewashed tollhouses, an absolutely amazing brick tunnel, and working canal boats, to name a few. To top it off, the canal and its towpath visit some of the nation's most charming little towns—including Harpers Ferry and darling Shepherdstown—as well as dozens of Civil War sites. Whether you decide to travel its entire 184.5 miles or just take a mile-long wander, you can't go wrong.

The C&O dates back to a time when canals were the proven apex of transportation technology, when the Erie Canal reigned supreme. As President John Quincy Adams turned the first shovelful of dirt in 1828, it was given that the canal would provide the quickest, cheapest method of transporting goods between the Chesapeake Bay and the vast Ohio Valley. But on that same fateful day, a similar ceremony was taking place in Baltimore, for the inauguration of the new-fangled railroad. Railroads in America were unproven as of yet, but before long it became clear that the C&O's fate was challenged by the Baltimore & Ohio Railroad—which one would reach the Ohio Valley first was anyone's guess.

Before long, labor shortages, unbelievably difficult terrain, constant funds shortages, and the unavailability of construction materials slowed the pace of canal building. Alas, it took the canal twenty-two years to reach Cumberland—eight more than the B&O. The railroad had thereby rendered the canal obsolete, dashing all plans to build any farther.

Nevertheless, the C&O—the nation's sixth largest canal—operated for nearly seventy-five years, carrying goods between the Alleghenies and Washington, D.C., opening up the Potomac River Valley. After the devastating 1889 flood, the canal went into receivership with the B&O, and the 1924 flood finally did it in. The canal was acquired by the National Park Service in 1938 and, after much soul-searching, the park service proposed to build a scenic parkway along the river. Thank goodness, Supreme Court Justice William O. Douglas recognized the recreational value of the canal and its towpath, and challenged journalists to take a walk with him in 1954 along its entire length. "One who walked the canal its full length could plead that cause with the eloquence of a John Muir," he wrote. Saved by popular appeal, the C&O became a national historical park in 1971 and one of Washington's most beloved playgrounds.

The first thing you have to do is decide exactly what you're going to do. Many people enjoy biking or hiking the C&O's entire length from Cumberland to D.C. (or vice versa), camping out at riverside sites, or staying in bed-and-breakfasts along the way. Some people bike the whole thing in two or three days (with the record being eighteen hours), although a more leisurely pace, one that offers the chance to take in some scenery and sites, is a week. Otherwise, you may decide to walk or bike just a segment. Georgetown to Great Falls, Edwards Ferry to Whites Ferry, and Harpers Ferry to Shepherdstown are some of the more popular biking jaunts, while you can't go wrong with a stroll near Great Falls or Harpers Ferry.

This narrative takes you from the canal's watergate in Georgetown to its last lock in Cumberland, from milepost 0 to 185. So start at the trailhead, located at the edge of Rock Creek Parkway, between Pennsylvania Avenue and Whitehurst Freeway. You begin along a row of Colonial-style houses, past one of the canal's most concentrated series of locks. From mid-April to mid-October, a

The Potomac River dances around boulders at Great Falls, along the C&O Canal.

FLOODS

Noah had his forty-day flood, but the C&O Canal has suffered through 170 years of overwatering—with no end in sight. About a year after construction began in 1828, floodwaters rose 64 feet at Great Falls, hugely impeding the work schedule. A flood in 1889 tossed boats like matchsticks, causing $100,000 worth of damage and forcing the canal into receivership. The final blow came when another flood hit in 1924, forcing the canal out of business forever. In recent years, a flood in 1985 caused $20 million in damages, while repairs from the 1996 flood are still under way. Every time another flood hits, the debate swirls about whether it's worth fixing and refixing this tiny fragment of history.

So what's the deal? Why so many floods? Simply because the canal was built on the Potomac floodplain. Planners knew that the river's narrow bed, with its steep banks, was ideal for a canal route. Alas, it's this same setup that makes the canal so vulnerable.

On the brighter side, all this flooding does wonders to the area's flora and fauna. A thin strip of limestone- and calcium-rich land, the floodplain is constantly swept with rich silt that nurtures a profusion of plants. Green ash, box elder, and hackberry are among the star trees that thrive here, while moisture-loving bluebells, trillium, and jack-in-the-pulpit burst into a frenzy of color in springtime. Rich plant life in turn lures a cornucopia of animals, including red foxes, white-tailed deer, pileated woodpeckers, and opossums. And then there are the birds: The Potomac River is located on the Atlantic flyway, promising the sighting of all kinds of different species here throughout the year, including bluebirds, cardinals, buffleheads, and diminutive juncos. A veritable garden of Eden indeed.

replica canal boat takes visitors on a veritable 1870s ride through one of the locks, complete with mule power and costumed boat captain, crew, and mule tenders who sing songs and share the folklore of old canal days. The tours leave from Foundry Mall on Thomas Jefferson Street, N.W., a half block south of M Street. Call (202) 653–5190 for information.

Just beyond Key Bridge await the ruins of the 1,100-foot-long Alexandria Aqueduct, which carried canal boats across the Potomac to a branch canal that connected with Alexandria. Farther ahead, at mile 3.1, stands Fletcher's Boathouse, where you can rent canoes and bikes. Step down to the river's edge for a peaceful moment, where the languid waters lap upon wildflower-dotted shores. Anglers stand by in rubber boots, hoping for shad, perch, catfish, and striped bass. The structure behind the boathouse is the Abner Cloud House, the oldest existing structure on the canal. Completed in 1801, it operated as a mill.

The pathway now enters a calmer realm, with the riffling Potomac off to the left. Around milepost 12 you come to Widewater, popular among anglers and canoeists (and great blue herons). The small lake is actually part of the old river channel, which canal engineers opted to use in lieu of building a new canal. (A rocky breach 200 yards long requires that you carry your bike.) Just up the path, a short side trail leads to the Great Falls Overlook (no bikes), certainly one of the top panoramas in the Washington area, if not the entire East Coast. A boardwalk brings you across a couple of islands to the middle of the river, where you stand amid the icy spray of Great Falls, a tremendous torrent of water, churning, pounding, and roaring over car-size boulders. Six locks were required to drop canal boats 41 feet here in less than a mile. At the uppermost lock, the lockkeeper's house was built in 1829 and enlarged twice by 1831. With the expansion it became known as Crommelin House, a popular hotel operating through the nineteenth century. It now contains a visitor center and historical displays. A mule-drawn barge, filled with summer visitors, plies the waterway here as in Georgetown.

Beyond Great Falls the crowds thin, and the C&O takes on a more tranquil mood. Take time to look and listen for the canal's plentiful birds: pileated woodpeckers and Carolina chickadees, wood ducks and bluebirds. Wildlife along the canal is abundant too; you're sure to spy beaver, rabbits, white-tailed deer, and the occasional fox. Beyond Violettes Lock at milepost 22, the canal is dry and overgrown; from here on there are only short, isolated stretches of water at Big Pool and Little Pool, and from Town Creek to Oldtown.

Edwards Ferry, at mile 30.8, operated on the river from 1791 to 1836; now there's just a boat ramp and the stone remains of Jarboes Store, which supplied the boating community. Whites Ferry at mile 35.5 still operates, the last working ferry on the Potomac. It carries you (and your car) across to Virginia and Balls Bluff National Cemetery, site of a Civil War battle, and 4 miles up Va. 15, to historic Leesburg.

Once of the canal's most beautiful structures lies just up the way at mile 42.2, the 500-foot, seven-arched Monocacy River Aqueduct. Built of local white and pink quartz sandstone, its robust masonry celebrates the craftsmanship of Irish immigrants. Indeed, Confederates failed to blow it up during the Civil War.

The Baltimore & Ohio Railroad located its eastern switching yard in the little railroad company town of Brunswick (milepost 55); a railroad museum on West Potomac Street tells the story. Proceeding along, you come to historic Harpers Ferry (at mile 60.7 take the footbridge across the river). Cradled by misty blue mountains at the dramatic confluence of the Potomac and Shenandoah Rivers, this peaceful little town is most famous for abolitionist John Brown's raid on its arsenal in 1859. He planned to equip a guerrilla army to liberate slaves, but ended up getting caught and hung instead; his escapades, however, helped precipitate the Civil War. The National Park Service owns many of the restored buildings, which now contain small museums on nineteenth-century life here (including the reconstructed firehouse where John Brown holed up). Little shops and cozy restaurants make a perfect excuse to stop by for an ice-cream cone or ice-cold lemonade.

Closely hugging the billowing Potomac, the next section of canal is certainly among the loveliest, with the towpath generally in great shape. A leafy green jaunt soon brings you to the Antietam Creek Aqueduct (mile 69.4), probably the canal's best-preserved aqueduct.

At mile 72.8 you come to a huge bridge that leads across the river to Shepherdstown, West Virginia's oldest town, settled in the 1730s. Shops and restaurants border its tree-shaded main street, including the popular Yellow Brick Bank restaurant. If you take the road in the opposite direction, you come to the town of Sharpsburg, site of the Antietam National Battlefield. The bloodiest day of battle during the

The Potomac Edison power plant is located at Dam Number 5 on the C&O Canal.

Civil War erupted here on September 17, 1862, when some 23,000 soldiers were either killed or wounded. A side trip to this pastoral battlefield is highly recommended (though it adds at least 10 miles round-trip to your journey).

Ahead, the landscape takes on a wilder look as you approach the dry ridges and valleys of the Appalachians. Seemingly in synch, the towpath also becomes more rugged, with a coarse gravel base that makes it harder to pedal. Pass through the old canal town of Williamsport (mile 99.3) and past four locks located within a quarter mile of each other (hence their name, Four Locks), one of the few places the canal strays from the river. At mile 112.4 you come to Fort Frederick, built in 1756 to protect pioneers from warring French and Indians; a small museum and interpretive programs provide insight to the restored fort. (The parallel Western Maryland Rail Trail has just been completed, making a nice alternate route to Hancock. See Trail 9 for details.)

Two engineering marvels lie upriver at Big Pool (mile 112.4) and Little Pool (mile 120.1), small lakes used to canalize the river channel. Hancock, at milepost 124, is another little canal town, where many boating families wintered. The National Park Service operates a canal information center with museum exhibits on Main Street.

Heading into the mountains, probably the most geographically remote but beautiful section of the towpath, you come to Paw Paw Tunnel at mile 155.2, considered the canal's most impressive engineering feat. To avoid the sheer cliffs along the Maryland side of the river, engineers chose to take the canal 3,118 feet through a mountain, an endeavor that took nearly fifteen years to complete. Entering the tunnel's dark, dank maw, your muffled footsteps interrupt the tomblike silence, a far cry from canaling days, when mule tenders illuminated the gloom with gaslit lanterns and boisterous captains shouted for the right-of-way.

Nearing Cumberland, residential backyards signal the beginning of development creep. Near mile 175 you come to the turquoise-shuttered *Cumberland,* a veritable replica of a canal boat. In summer, be sure to step aboard to see where the captain and his family (and mules!) slept.

The canal ends unceremoniously at milepost 184.5, beneath a highway overpass in Cumberland. Nearby, the canal's Cumberland Visitor Center occupies (ironically) the old Western Maryland Railroad Station, built in the old canal basin. The station also houses railroad and industrial museums, and Allegany County's tourist office.

4   Gold Mine Loop Trail

Showing the quieter side of Great Falls, a portion of this winding, woodsy trail travels along an old trolley bed. Farther in the forest await teetering mining shacks dating back to the 1800s, when this land was alive with gold prospectors.

Activities:

Location: Great Falls Tavern section of Chesapeake & Ohio National Historical Park, north of Georgetown in Montgomery County, Maryland

Length: 4.2 miles round-trip

Surface: Natural

Wheelchair access: No

Difficulty: Easy

Food: Great Falls has a seasonal snack bar, near the parking lot.

Rest rooms: Behind the Great Falls Tavern, to the left of the trailhead.

Seasons: Open year-round. Spring brings budding trees and warbling migrants, while autumn showcases gold and orange foliage. A dense canopy is a refreshing escape in the heat of summer; winter can be chilly.

Access and parking: Great Falls has a huge parking lot. There is a $4.00 parking fee.

Rentals: No

Contact: Great Falls Tavern, Chesapeake & Ohio National Historical Park, 11710 MacArthur Boulevard, Potomac, MD 20854; (310) 299-3613.

• • • • • • • • • • • • • • • • • •

The churning, roiling waters of the Potomac are the set piece of Great Falls, one that has mesmerized visitors for centuries. As such, the park's quieter sibling—splendid wooded uplands laced with hiking trails—has usually been ignored. Here, all is quiet but for the drumming of a pileated woodpecker on a fallen log, the sweet song of a springtime warbler, the rustling of treetops tousled by a gentle breeze—a splendid spot for a hike indeed.

A century ago, these tranquil woods were etched with trolley tracks, bringing frolicking passengers here to enjoy the watery drama and to dine at the tavern. The trolley line, which connected with the Rockville line at Bradley Lane in Bethesda, was built by the Washington and Great Falls Railway and Power Company in 1912–13 to link affluent residents of the Congressional Country Club neighborhood with the District. From the country club, the line then continued on through the countryside to Great Falls, a one way trip of forty-three minutes. Through service ran for five years, with the spur being completely abandoned in 1921.

Today you can walk along the former trolley rail bed, along the Gold Mine Loop Trail in the Great Falls Tavern section of the C&O Canal National Historical Park. The park is located 14 miles upriver from Georgetown, off MacArthur Boulevard. Find the trail just behind the tavern (now a small museum and visitor center), marked by blue blazes. Right away you can distinguish the dikelike ridgeline where tracks once ran. Rangers say that the old trolley turntable is located along the yellow-blazed Lock 19 Loop trail, though I have yet to detect its precise location amid the undergrowth.

Leaving the rail bed behind, you come to a T-intersection, where

The first portion of the Gold Mine Loop Trail follows the old trolley bed.

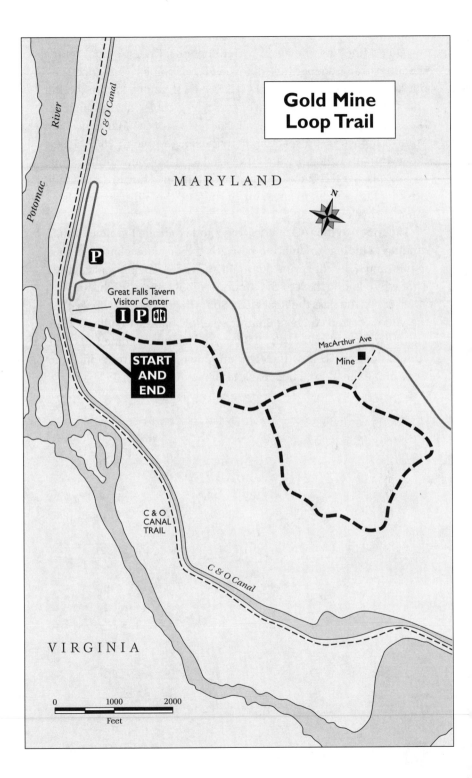

**Gold Mine
Loop Trail**

MARYLAND

Potomac River

C & O Canal

P

Great Falls Tavern
Visitor Center

I P

START
AND
END

MacArthur Ave

Mine

C & O
CANAL
TRAIL

C & O Canal

VIRGINIA

0   1000   2000

Feet

N

the Gold Mine Loop heads in both directions. Go left (you'll return the other way), deeper into the woods. You come to a branch trail, marked with a sign that says FALLS ROAD. If you go left up the hill you'll come across a collection of corrugated-roofed shacks, all leaning and dilapidated. These are all that remain of the Maryland Gold Mine, a hotbed of prospecting activities beginning in 1867. That's the year that a Union private purchased the lands here for the mine, having discovered traces of gold near Angler's Inn in 1861 while washing his mess kit in a stream. Farther up the hill, a sign explains some of this local history.

Backtrack to the FALLS ROAD sign and continue looping around, dipping, winding, undulating beneath the luscious canopy of oak, maple, and holly. In spring dogwood and redbud blooms add splashes of white and fuchsia to the scene, while warblers fill the air with sweet song. You pass the Rockwood Spur (to Rockwood School), then the yellow-blazed Angler's Spur, the yellow-blazed Woodland Trail, and the yellow-blazed Lock 16 Spur. And soon you come full circle around the loop. Follow the sign left, down the hill, retracing your steps along the old rail bed, back to the tavern.

5 Historic Savage Mill Trail

Beginning at the restored Savage Mill, this short, easy trail show-cases an exceptionally pretty section of the Little Patuxent River, its boulder-strewn banks speckled with anglers. Although bikers may find it a bit too short, families with strollers and wheelchair users will find it supreme.

Activities:

Location: The town of Savage, south of the Baltimore–Washington International Airport in Howard County, Maryland

Length: 0.5 mile one-way

Surface: Gravel ballast

Wheelchair access: Yes. The flat, smooth surface is ideal for wheelchairs.

Difficulty: Easy. Perfect for families with strollers.

Food: Savage Mill has a cafe where you can buy takeout sandwiches or sit down and eat.

Rest rooms: At Savage Mill

Seasons: Open year-round. Anglers flock to the riverbanks in spring in search of trout.

Access and parking: There is ample parking around Savage Mill.

Rentals: No

Contact: Senior Park Planner, Howard County Recreation & Parks, 7120 Oakland Mills Road, Columbia, MD 21046; (410) 313–4700.

• • • • • • • • • • • • • • • • • • • •

Given its short length, this simple trail should probably be listed as a minor rail-trail; but its course along the beautiful Little Patuxent River makes it an incredible find, one that shouldn't be tucked away.

To find the trailhead off I–95, just follow the signs for Savage Mill—it's in the town of Savage south of the Baltimore–Washington International Airport. On the banks of the Little Patuxent looms the great redbrick structure that once housed the Williams' textile weaving business. In 1820 the four Williams brothers borrowed $20,000 from their pal John Savage and named their enterprise after him. The mill mostly produced canvas: for the sails of clipper ships that sailed out of nearby Baltimore Harbor, for the cannon covers and tents of Civil War armies, for the backdrops of the first silent Hollywood movies. The mill operated until 1947, and has since been restored as an intriguing marketplace full of antique shops and arts and crafts studios—a really fun place to poke around.

In front of Savage Mill, walk across the Bollman Truss semi suspension bridge, built in 1869 and moved to this spot in 1887, when a spur of the Baltimore & Ohio Railroad was built to service the mill. It is one of the last standing such bridges in the world, recognized as a national treasure. On the other side of the Little Patuxent, turn right, onto the wide, smooth trail.

In the footsteps of anglers, no doubt, you traipse above the Little Patuxent River's left bank through wooded bliss. Across the way stand the foliage-draped remains of some of the mill's various outbuildings, ghostly reminders of bygone days. The river is gorgeous, riffling and billowing over smooth rocks, with overlooks now and again offering the chance for a better view. Your lofty vantage is a bit removed from the river, but little trails lead down to its boulder-strewn edge.

And that's about it. The path ends too soon in a wooded clearing. To return to the trailhead, reverse your route.

The Bollman Iron Truss Bridge spans the Little Patuxent River at the head of the Historic Savage Mill Trail.

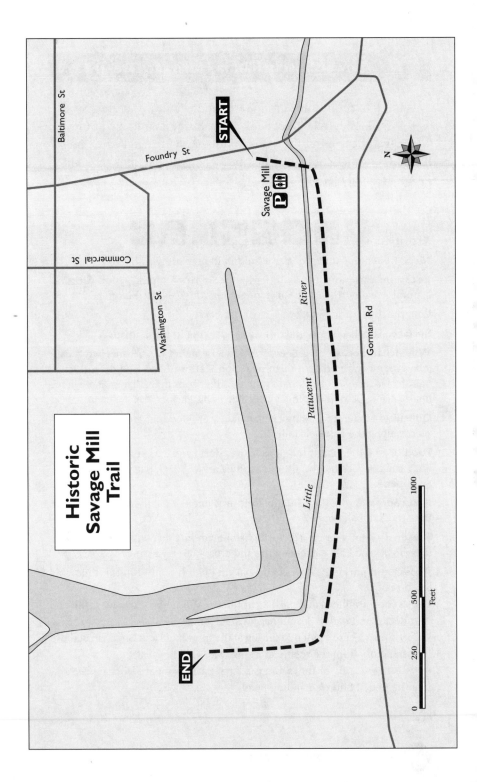

Historic
Savage Mill
Trail

START

END

Baltimore St

Foundry St

Commercial St

Washington St

Savage Mill

P

Little Patuxent River

Gorman Rd

N

0   250   500   1000
Feet

A favorite among birding diehards and wildflower enthusiasts, this trail follows the west bank of the Susquehanna River from the historic community of Rock Run to Conowingo Dam; along the way watch for bald eagles and other wildlife, plus rare and endangered blooms.

Activities:

Notes: Biking this trail requires a mountain bike or hybrid.

Location: Susquehanna State Park and Shure's Landing Wildflower and Natural Area, northeast of Baltimore in Harford County, Maryland

Length: 4 miles one-way

Surface: Crushed stone and dirt; wood decking in wetland areas

Wheelchair access: Yes. The 2.5-mile segment between Fisherman's Park (the greenway's northern terminus) and Stafford Road is wide and level; park at Fisherman's Park and enter the trail from there. There is a wheelchair-accessible portable toilet at Fisherman's Park.

Difficulty: Moderate. The trail is flat, but careful footing is required in rough places along the first half mile.

Food: The toll house at the Rock Run historic area has vending machines; Fisherman's Park has vending machines and a snack bar that is occasionally open.

Rest rooms: At the Rock Run historic area and the pavilion at Fisherman's Park (occasionally open)

Seasons: Open year-round. Spring is outstanding for its wildflowers; winter brings good bald eagle viewing and cross-country skiing.

Access and parking: Access and parking can be found in the following locations:

- *Rock Run:* Trailhead and parking at the Rock Run historic area, at the end of Rock Run Road in Susquehanna State Park.
- *Deer Creek:* There's pull-off parking at the mouth of Deer Creek on Stafford Road across from the trestle crossing Deer Creek.
- *Fisherman's Park:* At trail's end is a large parking lot at Fisherman's Park, at the end of Shure's Landing Road.

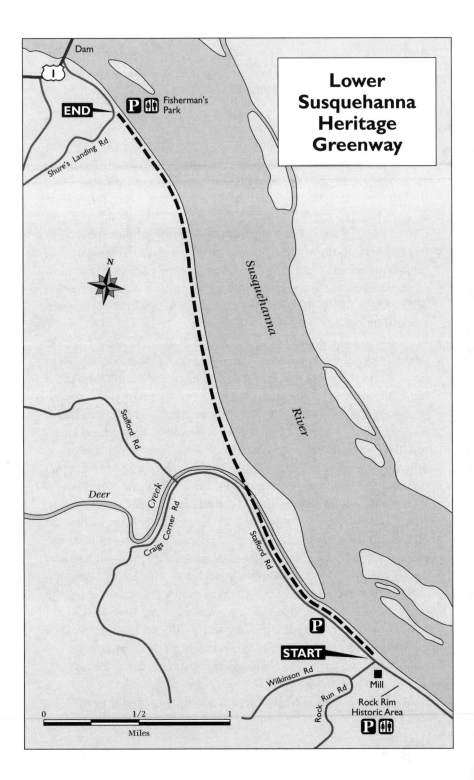

Lower
Susquehanna
Heritage
Greenway

Dam

END

Shure's Landing Rd

Fisherman's
Park

N

Susquehanna

River

Stafford Rd

Deer

Creek

Craigs Corner Rd

Stafford Rd

START

Wilkinson Rd

Rock Run Rd

Mill

Rock Rim
Historic Area

0   1/2   1
Miles

Rentals: No

Contact: Executive Director, Maryland Greenways Commission, 580 Taylor Avenue, Annapolis, MD 21401; (410) 974–3589.

• •

Soaring bald eagles are perhaps the most thrilling sight you'll see along this section of the Lower Susquehanna Heritage Greenway, but tens of thousands of blooming trillium, an old four story mill, the glorious Susquehanna River, and a rare daisy species are all here too. Tracing the Susquehanna's shoreline, you follow a portion of the former railroad right-of-way that the Philadelphia Electric Company built in the 1920s during construction of the dam that looms upstream. This trail is the first complete portion of the Lower Susquehanna Heritage Greenway, a proposed corridor of protected open space along both banks of the Susquehanna, with a 50-mile network of interconnecting trails.

You begin in the heart of Susquehanna State Park, along the river at the Rock Run historic area. The mile-long section between here and Deer Creek is not officially part of the greenway, although plans are in the works to make it so over the next couple of years. To find Rock Run off I–95 north of Baltimore, take the MD–155 exit at Havre de Grace and go north, following signs for the Steppingstone Museum. Beyond the museum, turn right on Rock Run Road and proceed down to the river. The first thing you'll probably spot is the picturesque old mill with its twelve-ton water wheel. Built in 1794 by local businessman John Stump, it operated until 1954 (with demonstrations now on summer weekends). Related structures include an eighteenth-century miller's house and carriage barn, a detached privy, a springhouse built in 1794–1804, and the thirteen-room manor house, completed in 1804. But the most interesting building is probably the white-frame toll house, where managers collected tolls to cross the mile-long bridge that once spanned the river here. Fire, vibrations caused by animal herds, and ice floes destroyed parts of the bridge, which closed in 1856. Out in front of all this, along the river, is the rail-trail. Turn left, heading upstream, along a short section of gravel surface.

A platform for wildlife observation is on your right, perfect for gazing out at the hundreds of birds that crowd the airspace above the sparkling waterway. Throughout your trek, keep scanning the river for a variety of gulls and herons, kingfishers, wood ducks, geese, and mallards. But the crowd pleaser is, of course, the bald eagle. There's at least one nesting pair in the area, meaning you may spot an eagle any time of year. But come winter, when the dam lures birds with ice-free water, many more come to feed, luring birders all along the riverbank, binoculars plastered to eyes.

Just beyond the observation platform, the trail deteriorates to dirt, following the old railroad tracks still crossed with ties; you'll have to watch your step as you negotiate the overgrown, uneven path. The great river is so close you can hear the lapping of its waters upon the muddy shore, the squawk of gulls circling for fish, the chatter of anglers waiting patiently for a bite.

In a quarter mile or so you come to the remains of an old stone aqueduct, providing a glimpse at the railroad's former incarnation. The rail bed was built along the route of the Susquehanna and Tidewater Canal, an important trade link between Pennsylvania and the Chesapeake Bay from 1840 to 1894. This 25-foot aqueduct, one of three along the canal, was constructed inexpensively of stone and wood (which is why so little remains today). Farther along awaits a trestle across the mouth of Deer Creek, and another glimpse at the railroad's past life. In canal days, a 246-foot-long dam here raised the creek level and supplied water for the canal downstream. A three-span wooden towpath bridge crossed the creek near the dam. Examine the stream for the remnants of both dam and bridge.

Across the current bridge, built for the railroad spur, the trail is now officially part of the greenway. It ducks into the woods of a narrow peninsula, with the Susquehanna to one side, Deer Creek

John Stump's mill, built in 1794, is one of the picturesque sights in Susquehanna State Park.

on the other. Soon, rocky, tree-covered slopes rise on the left, with a lush fertile floodplain (and the ever-present Susquehanna) on the right. This scenery may be unexceptional much of the year: short, scraggly trees, tangles of honeysuckle, plenty of mud. But in early April the floodplain brightens with hundreds of Virginia bluebells—a dazzling sight indeed. Then in mid- to late April the hillside transforms into a garden of springtime blooms that accompanies you to trail's end. The most precocious flower is the trillium, hundreds of thousands of them putting on one of Maryland's most spectacular wildflower displays. Their petals are white but these trillium are actually a rare form of red trillium. Joining them are Dutchman's-breeches (uncommon in Maryland), dogtooth violets, spring beauties, and wild ginger. Showy asters and goldenrod follow in summer and fall. The whole area is preserved as the Shure's Landing Wildflower and Natural Area, known for the rare and endangered plant species that thrive here, including several colonies of ferns and an endangered daisy species. As the early flowers fade, the woods become noisy with birds; early spring is peak spring migration for warblers, who follow the river north. Ospreys also arrive in spring.

About 3 miles from Deer Creek, in the shadow of Conowingo Dam,

Aqueduct ruins speckle the Lower Susquehanna Heritage Greenway. In the distance, stairs lead to a wildlife observation platform overlooking the Susquehanna River.

the trail ends at Fisherman's Park, complete with rest rooms and a picnic area. For one last hurrah, stroll over to the base of the dam, at the north end of the lot, where anglers drop their lines. Then turn around and enjoy it all anew.

7   Northern Central Railroad Trail

Wandering through stream-laced woods past farmhouses and fields of corn, this fine rural trail, part of Gunpowder Falls State Park, remembers the past with old railroad crossings and wayside hamlets brimming with stately architecture.

Activities:

Notes: Biking this trail requires a mountain bike or hybrid.

Location: From Ashland to the state line, northwest of Baltimore in Baltimore County, Maryland

Length: 19.7 miles one-way

Surface: Crushed stone

Wheelchair access: Yes, although the surface can become muddy after heavy rain.

Difficulty: Moderate. The first 10 miles north of Ashland are quite flat, but the section beyond Parkton has a gradual incline.

Food: The general store at Monkton (7.5 miles) has snacks; otherwise, the trail is pretty remote. It's advisable to pack snacks and water.

Rest rooms: Rest rooms or portable toilets at Phoenix, Sparks, Glencoe, Monkton train station, White Hall, Bentley Springs, and Freeland.

Seasons: Open year-round. The trail is chilly in winter months, with occasional snow good for cross-country skiing. In summer, the thick canopy shades you from the beating sun, but you will have to share the trail with many other outdoor enthusiasts.

Access and parking: Parking space is limited; on some weekends demand outweighs supply. The best tactic is to head north of Monkton, where it is less crowded. The following are some access points that have parking:

- *Ashland:* Take I–83 north to the Shawan Road exit toward Cockeysville; turn right on York Road, then left on Ashland Road for a half mile to dead-end at parking lot.
- *Paper Mill Road:* Take I–83 north to the Shawan Road exit toward Cockeysville; turn right on York Road, then right on Ashland Road. At Paper Mill Road bear left and look for parking on road shoulders.
- *Phoenix:* Take I–83 north to the Shawan Road exit toward Cockeysville;

turn left on York Road, then right on Phoenix Road. Proceed 1.7 miles to parking lot.

- *Sparks:* Take I–83 north to the Shawan Road exit toward Cockeysville; turn left on York Road, then right on Sparks Road. Proceed 0.7 mile to parking lot.
- *Monkton:* Take I–83 north to the MD–137 exit toward Hereford; turn right on York Road, then left on Monkton Road. Drive for 3 miles to trail crossing and parking lot. Parking is very limited here; users are encouraged to park in other areas.
- *White Hall:* Take I–83 north to the Middletown Road exit; turn right on York Road, then left on Weisburg Road. Follow Weisburg Road for 2 miles to parking lot at Weisburg and White Hall Roads.
- *Parkton:* Take I–83 north to the Middletown Road exit; turn left on Frederick Road and park at 18858 Frederick Road.
- *Bentley Springs:* Take I–83 north to the Stablers Church Road exit; take York Road north to Kaufman Road, turn left for less than a mile. Turn left on Bentley Road and proceed to parking lot.
- *Freeland:* Take I–83 north to the MD–439 exit; turn left on York Road and follow this to Freeland Road. Turn left and drive 2 miles to the parking lot.

Rentals: Monkton Bike Rentals, 1900 Monkton Road, Monkton, MD 21111; (410) 771–4058. Located across from Monkton Station.

Contact: Gunpowder Falls State Park, P.O. Box 480, 2813 Jerusalem Road, Kingsville, MD 21087; (410) 592–2897.

• • • • • • • • • • • • • • • • • • • •

Beginning amid the far-flung fingers of northern Baltimore's suburbia, the Northern Central Railroad Trail quickly sweeps you up into a rustic realm of icy trout streams, great old oaks and sycamores, and expansive fields and farms. Woodsy, remote, and incredibly serene, the trail ambles 19.7 miles from Ashland to the Maryland state line, where you have the choice of continuing on for another 20 miles through plush Pennsylvania countryside on the new York County Heritage Rail Trail. Along the way stand little hamlets where elegant architecture is the only memory of lucrative railroading days.

The Northern Central was one of the nation's few railroads built in the 1830s (completed in 1838, to be exact). Soon small towns dotted the countryscape to serve the line—Phoenix, Sparks, Monkton, Parkton, and Freeland among them. Flour, paper, milk and farm

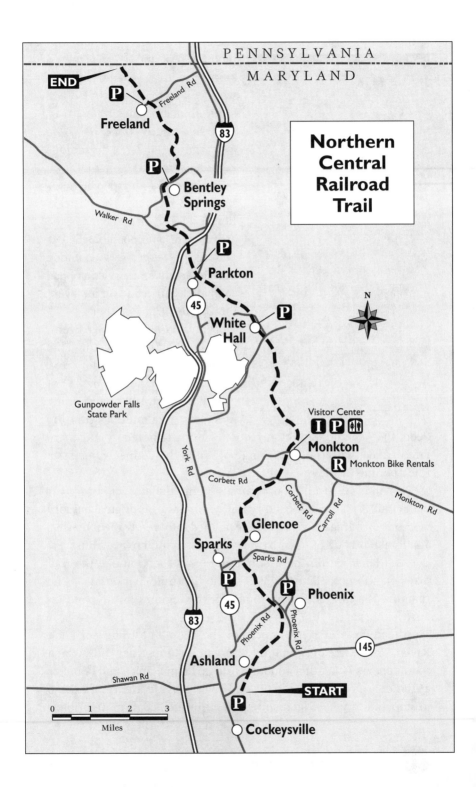

products, coal, and U.S. mail moved along the rails, as did soldiers wounded in the Battle of Gettysburg. Abraham Lincoln, too, traveled this route—once to go to Gettysburg to deliver his famous address (some say he wrote it on the train), and again upon being assassinated, en route to his burial in Illinois. Like so many railroads, the arrival of the automobile spelled its demise; passenger service ended in 1959, and freight service stopped soon after Hurricane Agnes swept through in 1972.

With a push from local citizens, the state of Maryland acquired the Northern Central corridor from Penn Central (the last owner of the railroad) in 1980, portending its success as a multiuse trail. Indeed, the Ashland–Monkton section was inaugurated to much fanfare in 1984, with the remaining portion to the Pennsylvania state line opening in 1989.

Ashland is the trail's southernmost point, the most crowded part of the trail. A nineteenth-century mill community, its original foundry workers' dwellings have been redeveloped into trendy town houses. You'll take off surrounded by new development, crossing busy Paper Mill Road within the first half-mile. But soon enough the trail takes on a remote, faraway feel. At the first mile marker stand the remains of a lime kiln, a reminder of the region's mining and industrial heritage.

Ahead on your right, watch for the deep blue waters of Loch Raven. The source of this pretty reservoir is Gunpowder Falls, which soon appears beneath a concrete bridge. Picnic tables and benches at the confluence of reservoir and river provide a perfect excuse to stop and, if you're so inspired, to bird watch (Baltimore orioles, cardinals, all kinds of ducks). Moving north, the trail runs beside the wide, meandering Gunpowder Falls, its chilly, clear waters harboring resident trout. Rubber-boot-clad anglers, some standing midstream, gracefully wave their lines in fervent hope of a bite.

At mile 2 you pass through the little town of Phoenix, first surveyed in 1793 by Elijah Merryman. Here loom the ghostly remains of the Phoenix textile mill. Purchased in the 1920s by the city of Baltimore as part of Loch Raven, it was demolished in preparation for the reservoir. But the water level never reached the mill, and so its ruins stand today.

The trail roams through woods and across Carroll Brook, popular with anglers for spring rainbow trout. The town of Sparks at mile 4 takes its name from early settler Laban Sparks—actually, from a switch station built here in 1835 that was named for Sparks, who owned a piece of adjacent land.

The next village you come to is Glencoe (around mile 5), a Victorian resort town once catering to well-to-do Baltimoreans wishing to escape the languid summer sun. The Glencoe Spring Hotel is long-gone, but other houses from that period still stand pretty. The following stretch to Corbett hugs the Gunpowder, providing watery vistas and plenty of good places to stop and relax. You'll notice that many of the trees along this trail have an odd narrowing at their bases, the work of apparently quite busy beavers. Just above mile marker 5, watch for the stone barn to the east, reminiscent of a bygone countryside.

Corbett (beyond mile 6) showcases fine Queen Anne houses, all of which grew up around a single building used as a general store, post office, school, and church; it's now a private residence. Farther north, undulating horse farms dot a scenic valley on the way to Monkton (mile 7.5), once one of the many railroad crossings along the railroad and now a major trail hub. The quaint old station houses a tiny historical museum and gift shop. Across the street, a general store now occupies the old Monkton Hotel.

Just above Monkton, the trail climbs along a rock face. The wide Gunpowder ever escorts you along, riffling over boulders, coursing through deep green pools. An occasional floodplain bursts in a riot of color with spring and summer wildflowers, while in winter ducks cavort in temporary ponds. Keep your eyes out for the cross section of a two-story structure, part of the stone remains of the old town of Pleasant Valley. By now you've probably noticed the signs marked W, posted sporadically along the trail. These indicate the old whistle stops, alerting engineers to blow their whistles for a road crossing.

At mile 9 Gunpowder Falls takes leave, replaced by sprightly Little Falls, heralding an especially beautiful section of the trail. Whitehall, at mile 10.8, is a former paper mill town that used the railroad to transport its paper to Baltimore. Just before reaching Parkton you come across a miniature waterfall: Little Falls splashing into an emerald pond.

Parkton, at mile 12.9, was a railroad hub for dairy products (hence this region's broad farmscapes). Take a break to wander the tiny town, to see its picturesque architecture and general store. Farther ahead, a parcourse edges the trailside, and you pass beneath Interstate 83. By mile 15, another stream has joined the journey: wee Beetree Run. Beavers thrive on the bounty of water here; given the number of fallen trees, they seem to be trying their best to dam the waterways. Around mile 15.5, you lose Little Falls, leaving Beetree Run alone to accompany you to the Pennsylvania border.

Beyond the old resort town of Bentley Springs (mile 15.7), once famous for its curative waters, the trail runs through a narrow stream valley, and then the land opens up with velvety valleys, rolling hills, and ruler-straight fields of corn. The scenery takes on a different look around mile 17, where, on the trail's west side, a little wetland harbors red maples and alders, cinnamon fern, skunk cabbage, and joe-pye weed.

Just beyond mile 18 lies the town of Freeland, with the trail's northernmost parking lot. Clapboard houses and mansard roofs are showcased along Freeland Road, hinting at the old railroad town's prosperity. From Freeland it's just 1.3 miles through an open valley to the Pennsylvania line—better known as the Mason-Dixon Line, the traditional demarcation between North and South. In fact, the first town across the border, New Freedom, was one of the first stops along the Underground Railroad where slaves were finally free.

From here you can continue north on the York County Heritage Rail Trail, which burrows through 10 more miles of lovely countryside to Hanover Junction; the last 10-mile stretch to York was scheduled to open in autumn 1999 (call York County Parks and Recreation Department at 717–771–9440 for updates and information). Otherwise, turn around and return the way you came. Going back, you're in for a pleasant surprise: The trail has a slight incline on its northerly route, making the southern journey virtually effortless.

Deciduous trees embrace the remote Northern Central Railroad Trail, near mile 17.

8   Number Nine Trolley Trail

This quiet, rustic trail along an old trolley route leads into a stream-crossed valley, far from the bustle of Ellicott City.

Activities:

Location: Between Oella Avenue in Ellicott City and Edmondson Avenue in Catonsville, just south of Baltimore in Howard County, Maryland

Length: 1.25 miles one-way

Surface: Asphalt, with a short segment of boardwalk

Wheelchair access: Yes, although there is a bit of a climb in the direction of Ellicott City to Catonsville.

Difficulty: Easy. The paved trail is a breeze for bikes and strollers, but a beginning child on a single-speed bike may find the uphill difficult.

Food: Ellicott City has restaurants.

Rest rooms: Howard County Tourism Council, 8267 Main Street (side entrance), Ellicott City.

Seasons: Open year-round. The valley attracts all kinds of bird migrants. Winter snowfall makes it a fleecy wonderland.

Access and parking: There are ample parking lots in Ellicott City, some free, some metered. The trail begins from Parking Lot A on Oella Avenue, but it is often full.

Rentals: No

Contact: Howard County Tourism Council, 8267 Main Street, Ellicott City, MD 21041; (800) 288–8747.

• • • • • • • • • • • • • • • • • • • •

The historic railroad town of Ellicott City is renowned for its little granite train station—the nation's oldest. Built in 1830, it was the first stop along the nation's first railroad, the Baltimore & Ohio. Still, the rail-trail that we're after here is actually along an old trolley line. In the turn-of-the-century heyday of electric streetcars, the #9 Trolley transported passengers from Catonsville (connected to Baltimore via another trolley line) to Ellicott City. Built in the 1890s, the trolley ran until 1955, when automobiles had clearly eclipsed its effectiveness.

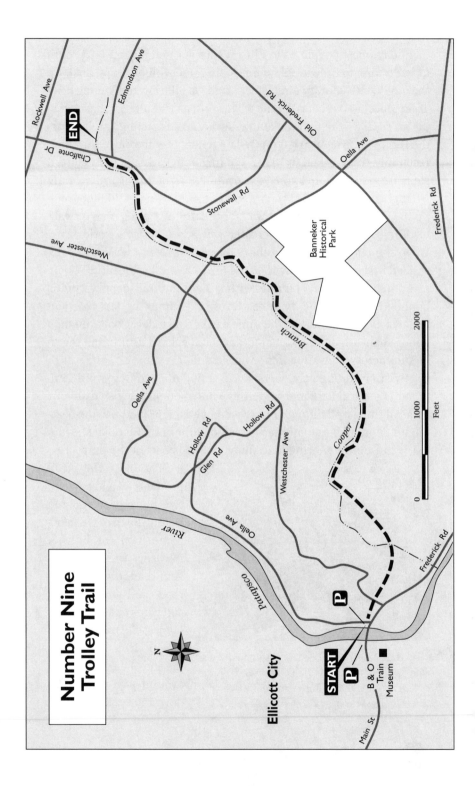

Number Nine Trolley Trail

N

Ellicott City

END

START

P

P

B & O Train Museum

Main St

Patapsco

River

Oella Ave

Glen Rd

Hollow Rd

Hollow Rd

Oella Ave

Westchester Ave

Westchester Ave

Cooper

Branch

Banneker Historical Park

Stonewall Rd

Oella Ave

Frederick Rd

Old Frederick Rd

Chalfonte Dr

Rockwell Ave

Edmondson Ave

Frederick Rd

0   1000   2000
Feet

Today, most people go to Ellicott City, located just off I–95 south of Baltimore, to browse its quaint Main Street full of shops, soak up the nineteenth-century atmosphere, and visit the award-winning B&O Train Museum (which is, by the way, worth a visit). But for those seeking an escape from the weekend crowds and congestion, stroll across the Patapsco River, turn left on Oella Avenue, pass the old Trolley Stop restaurant (established in 1833), and turn into Parking Lot A. Here, a staircase takes you up to the western trailhead of the #9 Trolley Trail

Right away you notice the impressive cut through a 100 foot rock ravine, hand-carved to make way for the trolley tracks. A boardwalk leads into a splendid, stream-crossed valley, seemingly a world away. Upon the opening of the trolley, this same sylvan enclave was described in the November 2, 1895, issue of *Argus:* "The beautiful Cooper Branch Valley . . . abounds with superb natural scenery, and is bounded on each side by dense forests." Despite the fact that you are neck-deep in suburbia, the same can be said today. Cooper Branch dances beneath oaks and maples, a woodpecker's drumming reverberates across the valley floor, warblers fill the air with song.

Twisting through the woods, the trail comes to Benjamin Banneker Historical Park and Museum, where you might wish to detour on a half-mile trail through pretty woodlands. This land was the eighteenth-century home and farmstead of America's first black scientist; a museum honoring his achievements is part of the park.

The B&O Museum in Ellicott City is housed in the oldest railroad station in the United States. In the distance sits the Trolley Stop restaurant, which once served trolley passengers.

The old trolley trail proceeds up a hill, where the houses of the old milling town of Oella become apparent, but not intrusive. You cross a private road, then another road, and continue for 400 yards or so past cozy homes with barking dogs. Edmondson Avenue is the end of the route. Turn around and enjoy the downhill back to town.

Winding along the Potomac River through rolling fields, woodlands, and rural towns, this new trail is a quick alternative to the parallel C&O Canal towpath.

Activities:

Location: From the town of Big Pool to Hancock, in Washington County, Maryland

Length: 10.7 miles one-way

Surface: Asphalt

Wheelchair access: Yes. The trail was designed specifically for wheelchairs.

Difficulty: Easy. The paved, nearly flat surface is a breeze to walk or bike.

Food: Hancock has several restaurants and fast-food joints; check out Main Street.

Rest rooms: Portable toilets at Big Pool trailhead.

Seasons: Open year-round. The trail is chilly in winter months, with occasional snow good for cross-country skiing. Much of the trail is exposed to the beating summer sun.

Access & parking: Access and parking can be found at several locations:

- *Big Pool:* In Big Pool there's a forty-car parking lot. Take MD–56 exit off I–70, to 0.75 mile west of Fort Frederick State Park.
- *Hancock:* In Hancock you can park for free at the Park and Ride lot on MD–144. Take MD–144 exit off I–70 to the lot, located about half a mile from the trail. You can also park at the large, metered lot off Main Street; follow signs from MD–144 exit off I–70.
- *Little Pool:* Access also at the Little Pool section of the C&O Canal.

Rentals: Pathfinders Canoe & Bicycle, 8 South Pennsylvania Street, Hancock, MD 21750; (301) 678–6870. Open year-round, it can be found between the C&O and current rail-trail terminus in Hancock.

Contact: Park Manager, Fort Frederick State Park, 11100 Fort Frederick Road, Big Pool, MD 21711; (301) 842–2155 or (800) 825–PARK.

• •

Wedged between the C&O Canal towpath and I–70 for most of
its length, the Western Maryland Rail-Trail shoots from Big
Pool to Hancock, west of Hagerstown. Paved and relatively flat, the
trail is fast, offering a less scenic but speedy alternative to the towpath (in-line skaters love it). This 10.7-mile segment, the first bit of
a planned 22.5-mile route, was completed in March 1998; trees beside it are still young and some signs and fences are not yet installed.
Regardless, it's a fun trip, and despite the proximity of the interstate,
there's the chance to spot wildlife, especially white-tailed deer, and
all kinds of birds fluttering through the canopy.

Before the Western Maryland Railway was built, the little town
of Hancock was serviced by the Baltimore & Ohio, which ran on the
south side of the Potomac River, with freight and passengers being
ferried across. Beginning in 1857, the Western Maryland Railway
constructed a short line to connect Baltimore with the western counties of the Maryland piedmont. Thanks to the generous funds of rail
baron George Gould, an extension was built into the coal-rich areas
of the Allegheny Plateau in Maryland and West Virginia. This "Cumberland extension," a portion of which is today's rail-trail route, was
completed between Big Pool and Cumberland in 1906. With the coming of the railroad, Hancock blossomed; much of the architecture
you see today dates from that era.

After World War I, daily traffic along the line comprised two or
three freight trains (loaded with coal going east, iron ore heading
west to Pittsburgh), a passenger train in each direction, and a local
commuter. The acquisition of twelve class 4-8-4 steam engines after
World War II, to help older steam engines in mile-long freight move-
ments, earned the line the nickname "Fast Freight Line." Over time,
the Chesapeake & Ohio Railroad (now owned by CSX) came to own
both the old B&O and the Western Maryland, eliminating the need
to operate both tracks; in the 1970s, the Western Maryland was thus
abandoned. The Department of Natural Resources acquired the 20.3-
mile abandoned right-of-way in 1990, and work on the multiuse recreational trail has progressed ever since. Plans call for eventually
expanding this section 10 miles, all the way to Pearre.

The Big Pool trailhead is conveniently located at a big parking
area just off I–70, on MD–56 about 0.75 mile west of historic Fort

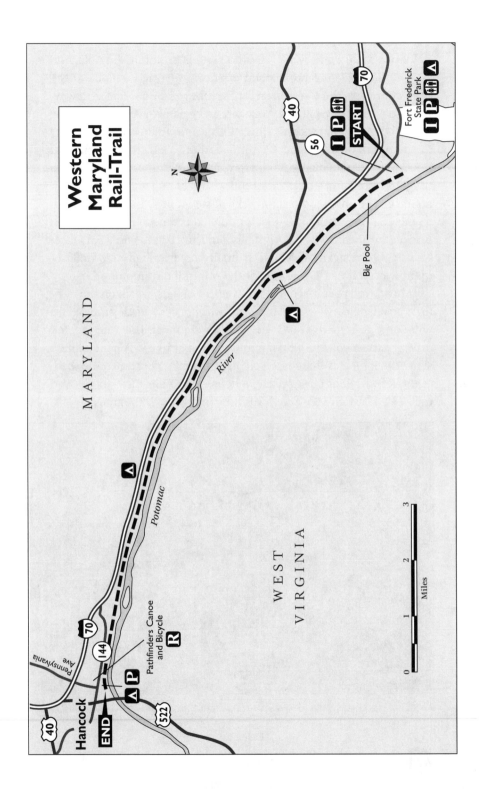

Western Maryland Rail-Trail

N

MARYLAND

WEST VIRGINIA

Potomac

River

Big Pool

Fort Frederick State Park

START

END

Hancock

Pennsylvania Ave

Pathfinders Canoe and Bicycle

70

144

40

522

70

40

56

0   1   2   3
Miles

Frederick State Park, which, by the way, is an interesting place to visit. Built in 1756 to protect settlers from warring French and Native Americans, the restored fort still evokes a frontier feel. Anyway, you can't miss the trailhead. You start off beside Big Pool, a mile-long natural depression that was filled with water and used by the C&O Canal to turn boats. As for the railroad, there aren't many signs that it was ever here. During its heyday, a coal chute, a water tower, a freight station, and a train order office stood here, but they have left no trace. The only memories are the adjacent B&O tracks still in use by the CSX line. In about a quarter mile you come to Ernstville Road Bridge, faced with stone. Originally built in 1930 to carry cars safely over the Western Maryland, it finally deteriorated; this replacement was built in 1997 as part of the rail-trail development.

Ahead, you pass through a farming crossroads; watch on the right for a post labeled W—indicating this was once a whistle stop. When you come to a road, you'll see another signpost, this one labeled B106, meaning you are 106 train miles from Baltimore. A handpainted sign here indicates there is a "cold pop" machine just down the road, to the left. Kind of out of place, a house next door raises emus and rabbits—watch for the large birds bobbing through the trees.

A CSX locomotive joins the Western Maryland Rail-Trail along the beginning portion

The trail proceeds through pretty farmland dotted with black-and-white cows, then enters woods speckled with old, rotting railroad ties. In the moister environment to the left (south) flourish box elders, red maples, and sycamores, while along the drier, north side grow red oaks, hickories, and early successional species. In spring, the trail bursts into color with redbud and black cherry; summer brings the sweet fragrance of honeysuckle.

Beyond sign B107 you cross a bridge over a pretty stream. What's interesting here is its proximity to the bridge on the left, for the C&O Canal, and to the bridge on the right for I–70. In just a stone's throw you have three different eras of transportation—the canal having been made obsolete by the railroad, and the railroad having been made obsolete by the car. From here to Hancock, you stay fairly close to the interstate, the roar of cars serving as a constant reminder of their dominance.

At the B108 marker, a small, forgotten cemetery hides in the tangled woods, its crumbling tombstones dating from the 1800s. Members of the Bryan, Long, Moor, and Snyder families lie buried here, early settlers who lived in the area, then called Park Head. Continue along, with rocky cliffs occasionally rising from the trail's north

of its modern-day incarnation, a fast, flat route through stream-riven woods.

An old C&O bridge can be seen from the Western Maryland Rail-Trail.

side, and pretty views of the Potomac River to the south (at least in leaf-free winter).

In a couple of miles you reach the former site of Millstone, an old canal town and village stagecoach stop along the National Road. During the Civil War, soldiers were stationed here to protect the canal from Confederates; in 1909, the town had one hundred people, along with a general store and post office, a harness maker, a distiller, a mason, several carpenters, and a teacher and blacksmith. Nothing remains of their history.

Around the B112 marker sprawls another large body of water, this one called Little Pool. Constructed for the C&O Canal, it was formed by transferring the towpath from the mainland to an island, with stop gates built at both ends to retain the water. Boats used it to turn around and to transfer freight. A staircase descends and crosses Little Pool to the towpath, making for a pretty diversion. Beyond B113, watch for a large brick building: the warehouse for Hepburn Orchards. This region is known for its peaches, apples, and grapes; a market around the side of the building sells some of this refreshing seasonal produce, including cider and pies. There are rest rooms here too.

At the B115 marker you enter the town of Hancock, the backyards of its pastel houses lining the trail's north side. Now just an afterthought off the interstate, this sleepy place once bustled with railroad, canal, and National Road goings-on. Relics at the Hancock Historical Society Museum (126 West High Street; open the second and fourth Sunday afternoon, April through October) help picture those glory days. Just ahead, the remains of a wooden railroad siding, worn and crumbling, lie off the trail to the left.

The trail dead-ends—for now, at least—beyond the rail-trail parking area. If you have the time, consider taking the C&O Canal back to Big Pool—although it's 5 miles longer, the riverside journey is especially quiet and bucolic. When you reach Fort Frederick, take the road up through the park, turn left on MD–56, and return to the parking lot, about 0.75 mile down the road. You can also cross back over to the Western Maryland Rail Trail at C&O mile markers 117 and 119.

MORE RAIL-TRAILS

Point Lookout Railroad Trail

Seemingly at the end of the world, Point Lookout State Park perches at the breeze-slapped point where the Potomac flows into Chesapeake Bay. Offering all kinds of water-based activities, the park is not really known for its rail-trail, a tiny little thing leaving from the visitor center. If you're in the area, however, it makes for a nice woodsy stroll.

The trail dates back a hundred years, when a railroad was planned to transport goods and people between Washington, D.C., and Point Lookout. The rail beds were all cleared but, due to a confusing medley of changing owners, the railroad never made it all the way to Point Lookout. The trail now exists thanks to the efforts of a local Girl Scout; hopes are high to extend it farther.

To reach the park from Washington, D.C., take MD–5 south about 70 miles to the end of the point.

Activities:

Location: Point Lookout State Park, St. Mary's County in southern Maryland

Length: 0.4 mile one-way

Surface: Clay and gravel

Wheelchair access: Yes

Difficulty: Easy

Food: No

Rest rooms: At the visitor center

Seasons: Open year-round. Summer is crowded with water and nature enthusiasts; the park is much quieter in spring and autumn.

Access and parking: Park at the visitor center.

Rentals: No

Contact: Ranger, Point Lookout State Park, P.O. Box 48, Scotland, Maryland 20687; (301) 872–5688.

Brandywine Rail-Trail

Paralleling the Brandywine River through beautiful Brandywine Park in downtown Wilmington, Delaware, this trail-in-progress follows the abandoned rail corridor of the Brandywine Branch of the Philadelphia, Baltimore, and Wilmington Railroad. When completed, the trail will connect to a network of other trails, including the Northern Delaware Greenway and the East Coast Greenway.

Activities:

Location: City of Wilmington, Delaware

Length: Currently 1 mile one-way. Another 1.5 miles is expected to be improved and open for use within the next year.

Surface: Paved

Wheelchair access: Yes

Difficulty: Easy

Food: Available in town a short walk away.

Rest rooms: Available in Brandywine Park.

Seasons: Warm days in spring and fall are ideal, when the trail is brightened with blooming flowers or changing leaves. Summer can be hot and humid, and winter is cold with various precipitation.

Access and parking: Access and parking in Brandywine Park. Park at the Brandywine Zoo Parking Area on North Park Drive.

Rentals: No

Contact: Delaware State Parks, 89 Kings Highway, Dover, Delaware 19901; (302) 739–5285.

Pomeroy Line Rail-Trail

The Pomeroy Line Rail-Trail links the city of Newark, Delaware to White Clay Creek State Park and the Mason and Dixon Trail. A portion of the rail-trail also serves as the westernmost section of the Northern Delaware Greenway.

Activities:

Notes: Mountain bikes or hybrids are recommended for biking.

Location: City of Newark, Delaware

Length: Currently 2.75 miles one-way. The trail is expected to be expanded southward into the central business area of Newark and to the University of Delaware campus area. Construction on the trail bridge crossing White Clay Creek is expected to begin soon, with completion scheduled for spring 2000. This bridge will connect portions of the trail on the east and west side of White Clay Creek.

Surface: Crushed stone

Wheelchair access: No. However, a handicapped accessible access trail is expected to be constructed in late fall 1999 or spring 2000.

Difficulty: Moderate. Though the terrain is relatively flat, the surface is slightly challenging.

Food: Available in Newark.

Rest rooms: Available in White Clay Creek State Park.

Seasons: Warm days in spring and fall are ideal, when the trail is brightened with blooming flowers or changing leaves. Summer can be hot and humid, and winter is cold with various precipitation.

Access and parking: The best place to access the trail is at White Clay Creek State Park; park at the nature center. Users can also access the trail from Newark, but currently there are no designated parking areas.

Rentals: No

Contact: Delaware State Parks, 89 Kings Highway, Dover, Delaware 19901; (302) 739-5285.

VIRGINIA

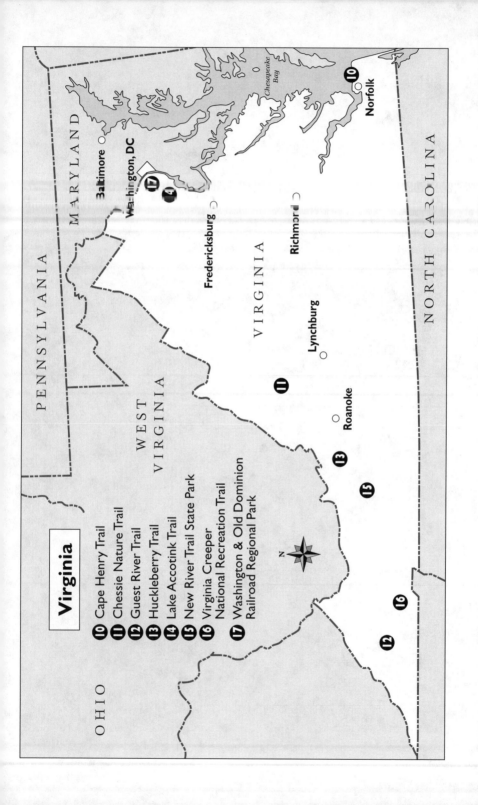

INTRODUCTION

The railroading era dawned as early as 1811 in Virginia, only to be confronted with the challenge several decades later of the Civil War. Indeed, the Orange & Alexandria, the Washington & Old Dominion (then called the Alexandria, Loudoun & Hampshire), and other railroads became major points of strategic contention as they transported troops and military supplies from front line to front line. Today, the rights-of-way of some of these lines have been converted into such marvelous rail-trails as the Lake Accotink Trail in northern Virginia, a popular route around a pretty lake, and the Washington & Old Dominion Railroad Regional Park, a 45-mile-long greenway connecting suburban Arlington with the rolling pastureland of Loudoun County. These trails hold valuable pieces of the nation's history, but you'd never know it as you travel along the scenic paths, listening to chirping birds and watching beavers putter across pristine ponds.

After the Civil War, people's attention reverted to more mundane things, like making money. Much obliging, the mountains of southwestern Virginia revealed huge resources of coal and timber. The most efficient way to haul them out? By train, of course. Thus was born the Huckleberry line between Blacksburg and Christiansburg, to transfer coal from Price Mountain; the New River line, connecting mining communities along the New River; and the Virginia Creeper, the fabled mountain railroad that carried timber off Whitetop Mountain and other soaring peaks. The legacy of those railroads is really fun rail-trails through some of the most beautiful, rugged countryside the East Coast has to offer.

All in all, Virginia has fewer rail-trails than one might expect in a state with so much history. Just remember that three of its eight major trails boast 30 miles or more, and that one, the W&OD, is among the nation's most utilized. Since there is no official statewide organization spearheading a rail-trail movement, the trails that exist are a credit to the efforts of individual organizations at all levels, from local to federal. Thanks to them, conversions are taking place all the time.

TOP RAIL-TRAILS

10 Cape Henry Trail (Main Trail)

The Cape Henry Trail winds through First Landing/Seashore State Park to Virginia Beach's oceanfront resort area, exploring a magical coastal environment of cypress swamps, bird-filled swales, exotic lagoons, and high sand dunes.

Activities:

Location: First Landing/Seashore State Park, in the city of Virginia Beach

Length: 6 miles one-way

Surface: Hard-packed sand and dirt

Wheelchair access: Yes.

Difficulty: Easy. The wide trail through the park travels across fairly flat terrain, although the section along the Narrows becomes narrower and has some deep sandy spots.

Food: The park has a camp store, and there are vending machines at the Narrows. You'll have to go into Virginia Beach for restaurants.

Rest rooms: At the park visitor center (at the trailhead) and at the Narrows (end of the trail)

Seasons: Open year-round. The trail gets lots of use during the warm weather of early spring through early fall; for privacy you may wish to visit early on weekend mornings or, even better, during the week.

Access and parking: The trail is accessible from two locations:

- *First Landing/Seashore State Park:* The park entrance is located on U.S. 60 in Virginia Beach. From I–64, take the U.S. 13 exit and follow this to U.S. 60. Go right for about 5 miles to the entrance. Turn right, into the park, and follow the entrance road to the visitor center and parking area. The trail begins just below the visitor center.
- *64th Street:* You can also access the trail on 64th Street, off Atlantic Avenue.

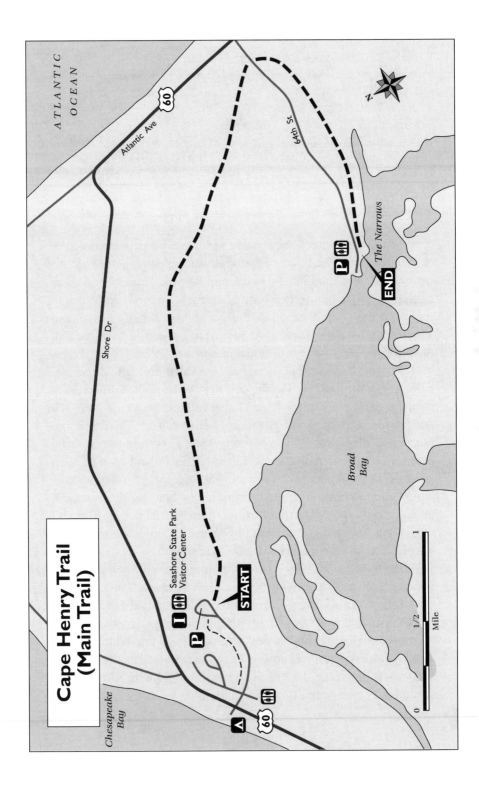

Cape Henry Trail (Main Trail)

ATLANTIC OCEAN

Chesapeake Bay

60

Atlantic Ave

Shore Dr

60

Seashore State Park
Visitor Center

P

START

64th St.

P

END

The Narrows

Broad Bay

N

0   1/2   1

Mile

Rentals: Rentals are available nearby:

- Seashore Bike & Hobby Shop, 2268 Seashore Shoppes, Virginia Beach, VA 23451; (757) 481-5191.
- Ocean Rentals Beach Service, 577 Sandbridge Road, Virginia Beach, VA 23456; (757) 721-6210.

Contact: First Landing/Seashore State Park and Natural Area, 2500 Shore Drive, Virginia Beach, VA 23451; (757) 481-2131. Department of Conservation and Recreation, Division of State Parks, 203 Governor Street, Suite 306, Richmond, VA 23219; (804) 786-1712

• •

F ar from the genteel, fox-chasing Virginia most people know, the Cape Henry Trail plies a Faulkneresque landscape of bald cypresses, ancient sand dunes, and green herons. This magical coast setting is First Landing/Seashore State Park, an emerald wedge of nature in the heart of bustling, tourist-flocked Virginia Beach, and Virginia's most popular park. As such, don't expect to have the trail to yourself—certainly not in midsummer.

It's hard to believe that trains once rumbled through this wilderness, but in the early part of the century the Norfolk Southern Railroad ran on portions of the Cape Henry Trail, linking Virginia Beach and Norfolk with the North Carolina cities of Raleigh, Charlotte, and Morehead City. Frolicking vacationers used the line to reach the oceanfront, where dance halls, saltwater pools, and casinos soon sprang up—the dawning of Virginia Beach's resort persona. Visitors and residents continue to enjoy strolling the boardwalk, munching on corn dogs and cotton candy, as much as they did in the 1920s and '30s. What has changed is the railroad itself, which has metamorphosed into this fabulous, nature-bound rail-trail.

The wide, flat trail begins from the park's visitor center, which you can access via U.S. 60 in Virginia Beach, about 3 miles east of the Chesapeake Bay Bridge. You enter an enchanted forest of bulbous-based bald cypresses, their gnarled branches draped in Spanish moss and their knobby "knees" poking through tea-colored waters. This is one of the northernmost bald cypress swamps in North America, with some of the trees aged 600 years or more. In summer the ground may be nearly dry, and wildlife is seemingly scarce. But in spring, especially after a dousing rain, the dripping forest stirs with animals. Watch for painted turtles, pileated woodpeckers, green herons, snowy egrets, lizards, flying squirrels, snakes, and frogs. There are two elusive critters that you probably won't see: the prothonotory warbler, which is here spring through fall, and the chicken turtle, which lives nowhere else in Virginia, named for its amusingly long neck.

You roll the length of the park, passing by the Kingfisher Trail and the White Lake Trail, both choice opportunities to stroll (no bikes) among wildlife. The farther you go, the more the terrain resembles Virginia's old-growth forest of long ago.

Just beyond mile 3.8, cross 64th Street and go across a wooden bridge through cypress woods. You then come to a fork; go right (left leads to a contact station). You tunnel through a glorious stretch of great live oaks draped in Spanish moss, and soon spot glimmering blue water off to the left. That's the Narrows, beloved domain of ospreys and herons, black ducks and mallards. The trail becomes exceedingly sandy and twisty as you cross ancient dunes—some as high as 75 feet—sprinkled with pine, oak, and hickory. This portion of the trail is narrower and rougher, and soft sand in some places makes it difficult to pedal.

A boardwalk takes hikers and bikers across a bird-filled swale.

And then, just beyond mile 4, comes my favorite part: a board-walk across a sunny, bird-filled swale, where a salt marsh has dom-inated over piney woods. Birds love the dead trees: Nesting in the hollow trunks are pileated woodpeckers, tiny brown-headed nuthatch-es, and all the bird sizes in between. An observation tower allows you to stop and survey the scene. In late March to October, chances are good you'll spot an osprey nesting in the higher trees.

Farther along, you crest a hill, spot the shimmering waters of Broad Bay, and end at a parking lot amid boats, a pine- and oak-fringed little beach, crabbers, and fishermen.

If you're not tired of biking, you can take 64th Street east out of the park, turn right on Atlantic Avenue, and proceed 1.5 miles to the oceanfront boardwalk. From there, it's 2.5 miles along the coastline to Rudee Inlet, where the boardwalk ends.

Bikers take a break along the Narrows at Seashore State Park, where the Cape Henry Trail is the main biking path.

11 Chessie Nature Trail

This genteel trail along the Maury River features spectacular limestone cliffs, riots of wildflowers, wineberries growing in profusion, and reminders of both its canaling and railroading past.

Activities:

Location: Between Lexington and Buena Vista in central Virginia

Length: 7 miles one-way

Surface: Crushed cinders and dirt

Wheelchair access: Yes, for trail wheelchairs; obtain a key to the gates in advance.

Difficulty: Easy. The trail is wide and level.

Food: Groceries and restaurants in downtown Lexington

Rest rooms: No

Seasons: Open year-round

Access and parking: Currently there are three places where you can access the trail:

- *Old Buena Vista Road:* The footbridge across the Maury River has been washed away for now so you'll have to begin the trail at its second access, Old Buena Vista Road, about a half mile downstream. From downtown Lexington, follow U.S. 11 north to Old Buena Vista Road and turn right. In a half mile or so you'll see the trail access on the right.
- *Stuartsburg Road/South River:* You can also access the trail at its midpoint, where Stuartsburg Road crosses South River.
- *Stuartsburg Road/U.S. 60:* You can access the trail at its endpoint on Stuartsburg Road, just upstream from U.S. 60 and the city of Buena Vista.

Rentals: No

Contact: Lexington Visitors Center, 106 East Washington Street, Lexington, VA 24450; (540) 463–3777.

• •

A precious vassal of nature, the Chessie Nature Trail beckons with magnificent views of the Maury River, stunning limestone cliffs, luxuriant banks of wildflowers, and little sign of modern life. This lustrous, wineberry-scented corner is found in the county of Rock-bridge, between Lexington and Buena Vista.

Lexington is located on the North River—officially called the north branch of the James. It was renamed the Maury in 1945 in honor of world-famous oceanographer Matthew Fontaine Maury, who taught physics in town at the Virginia Military Institute (VMI) after the Civil War. Always an important market hub, Lexington was linked to Richmond in the 1850s with the James River and Kanahwha Canal. Then in 1880, in keeping with the times, the Richmond & Allegheny built tracks in place of the canal, giving birth to the line that would become known as "Chessie's Road."

The first train roared into East Lexington on October 15, 1881, and over the next eighty-eight years the line brought freight and passengers and VMI cadets in and out of town. Aside from the Richmond & Allegheny being absorbed into the Chesapeake & Ohio system, not much changed along the North River Branch until 1969. Then Hurricane Camille swept through, destroying trestles and most of the rail

One of the old cement cairns along the Chessie Nature Trail informed the train engineer that Balcony Falls lay 19 miles ahead.

bed. The exorbitant cost of repairs forced the C&O to abandon the line. In 1979, VMI bought the right-of-way with help from various groups, and began development of the nature trail.

Normally, Chessie Nature Trail begins on Jordan's Point, where the Great Road from the North (U.S. 11) crossed the river. The footbridge recently was washed out, however, so you'll have to access the trail about a half mile downstream. From downtown, follow U.S. 11 north to Old Buena Vista Road and turn right. In a half mile or so you'll see the trail access on the right.

You're not missing out on a lot by this closure; much of the

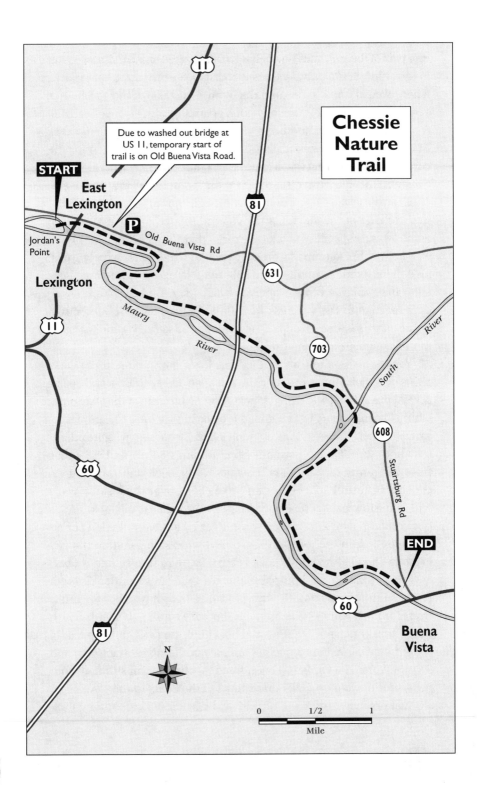

START

East
Lexington

Due to washed out bridge at
US 11, temporary start of
trail is on Old Buena Vista Road.

P Old Buena Vista Rd

Jordan's
Point

Lexington

Maury

River

Chessie
Nature
Trail

631

703

South River

608

Stuartsburg Rd

60

END

60

Buena
Vista

81

N

0   1/2   1
Mile

first part of the trail goes through the backyards of small industries. But if you want, you can walk the short distance upstream to the island, where Woods Creek flows into the Maury. Just above the confluence stands the mill race for the long-gone gristmill, dating from circa 1810. A saw mill, foundry, and forge were also here in the 1820s and '30s. About 200 yards downstream from the U.S. 11 bridge, watch for the concrete cairn bearing the cryptic BF 19. One of several posts along the way, It marks the train distance from this point to Balcony Falls.

Otherwise, heading downstream from the temporary trailhead in the shade of wonderful cliffs, you are treated to a convention of wildflowers, especially along the river's rocky banks. Look for bloodroot in March; Dutchman's-breeches and rue anemone in early April; blue phlox, wild columbine, and trillium in late April; and dwarf larkspur, fire pink, and May apples in early May. Birds, too, are abundant, thanks to the variety of habitats: water, steep wooded cliffs, fields, pastures, deep woods. The peak period is early May, when all the migrants are passing through.

You soon come to Clifton, the large brick house built in the early 1800s by Major John Alexander, the son of an early settler; it still boasts several plantation-style dependencies, a veritable taste of the Old South. On this lawn, Robert E. Lee joined crowds in watching the annual regatta between VMI and Washington College, where he was president.

About 2 miles downstream from Jordan's Point (and 1.5 miles from the temporary trailhead) awaits Reid's Lock and Dam, an especially beautiful spot. Vines and trees hang over thick stone walls where narrow packet boats once passed through. At the lock, mules (for freight boats) and horses (passenger boats) were ferried across the river, to join the towpath there. The wide stone shelf at the river's edge just below Reid's Lock is a perfect perch to sit and relax.

Proceeding along, you pass beneath I–81, and wander through pretty bottomlands dotted with plump rolls of hay. About 4 miles from Jordan's Point (3.5 from the temporary trailhead) stands South River Lock, one spot where canal boats left the river for a specially constructed canal in order to bypass the confluence of the North and South Rivers. The canal has been filled in, but you can still make out parts of the two-step locks that returned the boats to the river.

Just downstream, the South River Bridge is a 235-foot-long foot-

The mill race from the long-gone gristmill can still be seen on the Maury River, near the start of the Chessie Nature Trail at Jordan's Point.

bridge constructed on the old railroad bridge. Step across for fabulous blue-and-green views of the South River and surrounding bottomland, rich in wildflowers and bird life. About 100 yards farther downriver is the confluence of the Maury and South Rivers.

Farther on, look across the river for the Hidden House, which may be hard to make out May to November with the tree canopy. This 1850 Greek Revival brick residence, featuring a double portico, lay between the specially constructed canal and the river, so boats passed through its backyard along what is now a field. It's said that when Stonewall Jackson's body was carried from the Chancellorsville battlefield to Lexington in 1863, it followed a route through this field.

Not far from Hidden House, a W marked on a post once reminded engineers to blow their whistles (long, long, short, and a long blast) upon approaching the old public road (now VA–839).

About 6 miles below Jordan's Point (5.5 from the temporary trailhead), you come to the Ben Salem Lock and Dam. The dam is now just a jumble of rocks across the river, but the lock is well preserved. At this point the mules or horses pulling the canal boats were again ferried across to the left side of the river. Another lock, Zimmerman's Lock, lies less than three-quarters of a mile farther downstream. The trail continues from this point for less than half a mile.

12 Guest River Gorge Trail

Vaunting high rock bluffs, cascading waters, and hardwood forest, this rail-trail follows the Guest River through a magnificent sandstone gorge. Located in Jefferson National Forest, the area is isolated and remote—chances are you won't meet a soul.

Activities:

Notes: Mountain bike or hybrid required for the last 4.3 miles. Paddlesports along this trail include canoeing and kayaking.

Location: South of the town of Coeburn in Wise and Scott Counties of southwestern Virginia

Length: 5.3 miles one-way

Surface: The first 1.5 miles are hard-packed gravel, while the last miles are original gravel ballast.

Wheelchair access: Yes. The first 0.3 mile is wheelchair accessible.

Difficulty: Moderate. The trail follows a mild downhill grade from trailhead to trail's end; keep in mind the uphill return. The large, loose gravel can be hard for beginning bikers (and makes for a noisy bike ride).

Food: There is no food along the trail. Restaurants and groceries are located in the nearby town of Coeburn.

Rest rooms: At the trailhead

Seasons: Open year-round. Spring through fall is the best time of year. Winter can be extremely cold, but good for cross-country skiing.

Access and parking: You can only access the trail from its trailhead. From the town of Coeburn in southwestern Virginia, take VA–72 south for 3.9 miles to a paved access road (it's marked by a GUEST RIVER GORGE sign). Drive 1.3 miles to the parking area and trailhead.

Rentals: No

Contact: Clinch Ranger District of Jefferson National Forest, 9416 Darden Drive, Wise, VA 24293; (540) 328–2931.

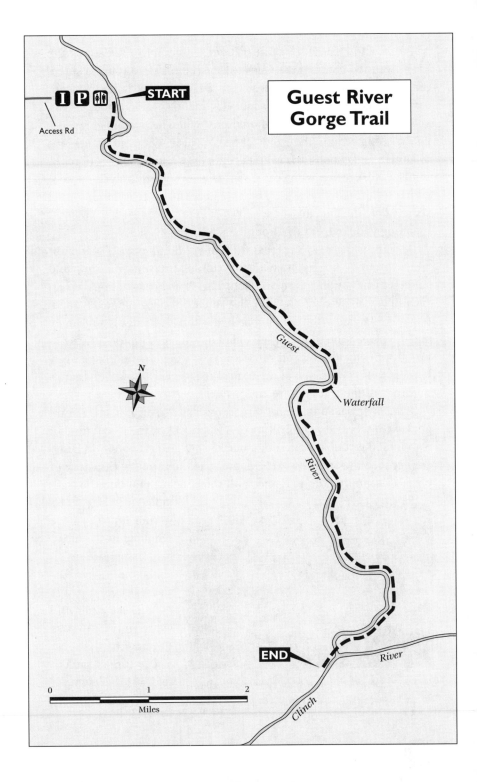

Wild and remote, the Guest River Gorge Trail rolls above the forested banks of the Guest River as it rushes through a splendid sandstone gorge—a perfect stage from which to watch translucent waters dancing around car-size boulders, spilling over long rock ledges, splashing down sudden elevation drops. When the water is high, the Guest River becomes the scene for some spectacular white-water runs in kayaks and canoes, while anglers are drawn to its bounty of trout. But chances are you won't see a soul as you travel this pretty route— a lone fisherman if anyone. The only downside is that the trail runs slightly downhill into the gorge—400 feet over the course of 5.3 miles— meaning you have to turn around and climb back out.

It was during the 1800s that the Norfolk Southern Railroad built a line through the gorge to haul coal (for heating and smelting) and saltpeter (for gunpowder manufacturing) from nearby mines. When the railway abandoned the line, the Forest Service accepted a donation of 5.57 miles of the old railroad bed within the Guest River Gorge, and developed the trail you see today. Local community groups envision building a hands-on museum near the gorge, perhaps overlooking the river off one of the high cliffs. For now, however, there's nothing but the trail, nature, and you.

The river beckons from the parking lot, its soft murmurs mingling with the incessant drilling of a woodpecker, the sweet tune of warblers, the rude outburst of a black crow. At first you're in heaven, because the trail is wide, smooth, and downhill, with plenty of pleasing scenery. You may mock all the benches that line the trail-

A hiker stops to enjoy the scenery near the Guest River's confluence with the Clinch River.

side; hold any judgments until you're climbing back out.

A brochure available at the trailhead describes several points of interest along the way. You soon pass through the first one, Swede Tunnel, built in 1922 by locals, some of whom were Swedish.

A biker crosses the bridge near the end of the trail.

Soon after, you come to the first, and longest, of the trail's trestles. The fabulous upstream views are your first glimpses of the gorge and its tree-cloaked cliffs.

About 1.5 miles into the trek you cross another trestle, over Crab Orchard Branch, and begin a bumpy ride on the loose gravel. It's not too bad to ride on, but it sure makes a lot of noise (hiking is much more tranquil). Farther on you pass beneath two large, jagged outcroppings, actually parts of the cliff that were blasted with explosives to make way for the rail line. The black spots are soot deposits left over from steam engines. Continue along, ever enjoying the river-and-forest vistas at every turn. Be sure to glance over your shoulder now and again to see what's upfolding upriver as well. Around mile 4 watch for a pretty waterfall on your left.

The trail ends at a trestle over the Guest River, just short of its confluence with the Clinch. You can't see the actual meeting point, which is blocked by a working railroad trestle. You can, however, enjoy the fabulous view to the other side of the trestle: the Guest waltzing beneath a dramatic cliff. Take one last look before heading back uphill, remembering that one advantage of the slower pace is the chance to examine the trailside wildflowers, especially beautiful in spring.

This absolutely gorgeous trail winds through plush pastures, quiet neighborhoods, and pocket woods in a region famous for its coal history.

Activities:

Location: Between Blacksburg and Christiansburg, in Montgomery County of southwestern Virginia

Length: 5.75 miles one-way

Surface: Asphalt

Wheelchair access: Yes. The entire trail is designed to be wheelchair accessible. Pulloffs are provided at intervals along sections of the trail where the slope is between 5 and 8.3 percent.

Difficulty: Easy. Most of the trail is level.

Food: There are a number of restaurants in downtown Blacksburg at that end of the trail. The New River Valley Mall (food court) is at the Christiansburg end. There is no food or water along the trail itself.

Rest rooms: Public rest rooms are only available at either end of the trail: in Blacksburg at the public library and in Christiansburg at the New River Valley Mall (food court).

Seasons: Open year-round. Spring is especially beautiful, with the blooming dogwood and redbud. Winter can be chilly, though occasional snow makes it an ideal cross-country skiing venue.

Access and parking: There is ample parking at either end of the trail:

- *Christiansburg:* To reach the Christiansburg trailhead from I–81, go north on U.S. 460 to Peppers Ferry Road, turn left, then turn right into the mall; the trailhead is off the loop road around the mall, near the Sears store.
- *Blacksburg:* To reach the Blacksburg trailhead from I–81, take U.S. 460 north to Miller Street and turn left into the Blacksburg Public Library; parking is allowed on nearby public streets, except where signs indicate otherwise.

If you want to access the trail midway, keep in mind that parking is limited. Possibilities include:

- *Virginia Tech campus:* On campus parking is available at the Tennis Facility on Tech Center Drive and at the Library Storage Facility located on

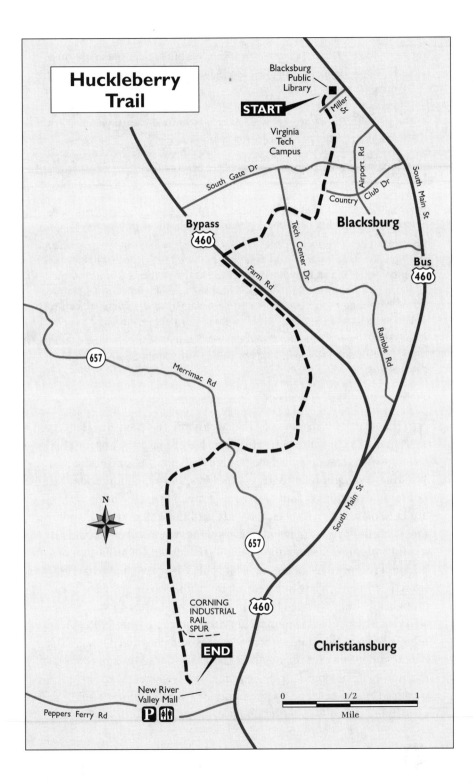

Country Club Drive Extension. A visitor permit is required to use these parking lots between 7:00 A.M. and 5:00 P.M. Monday through Friday. Permits are available on a daily or extended basis through the Visitor Information Center on South Gate Drive.

- *Mabry Lane:* There are a few parking spaces at the entrance to Warm Hearth Retirement Community on Mabry Lane.

Rentals: Rentals are available nearby:

- Hokie Sports, 101 South Main Street, Blacksburg, VA 24060; (540) 552–7765; rents bikes.
- Tangent Outfitters, c/o Java River Company, 1055 Norwood Street, Bradford, VA 24141, (540) 674–5202; arrange rentals ahead of time.

Shuttles: The "Two Town Trolley" (Blacksburg Transit) operates between the New River Valley Mall and downtown Blacksburg. The bus makes two pickups at the mall in the early morning and seven pickups at the mall in the afternoon on an hourly basis. All buses are wheelchair accessible. Buses equipped with bike racks can be assigned to the route by calling Blacksburg Transit (540–961–1185) at least a day in advance.

Contact: Planning Director, Montgomery County Planning, Annex Building, 4 South Franklin Street, P.O. Box 6126, Christiansburg, VA 24068-6126; (540) 382–5750.

• •

In the hazy blue shadow of Price Mountain, the slick Huckleberry Trail traces the route between Blacksburg and Christiansburg that steam-powered railcars once took, laden with precious anthracite coal. Winding through plush fields, wetlands, quiet neighborhoods, and pocket forests, this verdant greenway is much loved by locals. (If you are here on a sunny weekend, try to avoid the trail midday.) And be forewarned: There are several road crossings where bikers should dismount and carefully cross the street. Be that as it may, an early morning stroll is sure to unveil grazing white-tailed deer, songbirds chattering from the treetops, a shy frog peering from beneath murky waters, cottontails nibbling trailside clover, maybe even a turtle or two.

Price Mountain. The name still evokes images of the carbon-faced miners, yellow-and-white company houses, and piles and piles of black coal that dominated this region in the early 1900s. In fact, coal was taken from Price Mountain long before that. It was discovered in Montgomery County during the Revolutionary War by Hessian soldiers; over the next century, settlers built some of the nation's first blacksmithing operations—really not much more than open pits that pock-marked Price Mountain's lower slopes. As demand grew, coal was dug deeper and sent farther away. In the Civil War coal from here is said to have fired the boilers of the *Merrimac* during its ill-fated encounter with the *Monitor* at Hampton Roads (that's how the community of Merrimac got its name). Regardless, Price Mountain's coalfields weren't truly developed until the early 1900s, when a general strike by anthracite miners in Pennsylvania fueled the demand for Virginia coal.

Locals had long clamored for a railroad to connect them with the rest of the world, but it wasn't until this turn of events that the Virginia Anthracite Coal and Rail Company—a group of northern capitalists—laid tracks to transport coal from the Merrimac Mine near what is now Montgomery Regional Hospital to the Christiansburg railway station at Cambria. In 1904 the rail was extended from the mine to Blacksburg.

In addition to coal, passengers also traveled the line, including cadets from Virginia Tech. They are allegedly the ones responsible for the name "Huckleberry"; the train would often stall, and the cadets passed time by hopping off and picking trailside huckleberries. By the 1950s, the mine had closed and passengers were using cars more than trains. The Huckleberry made its last run in 1958.

Soon after, part of the train path was converted into a nature trail. This has since been augmented by Friends of the Huckleberry, who have worked closely with the governments of Blacksburg, Christiansburg, and Montgomery County to create the gorgeous rail-trail you see today. Work is under way to extend both ends.

Begin the trail on Miller Street in Blacksburg, next to the Blacksburg Public Library. The site of the old Temporary Depot (1904) is now part of the town parking lot, while the site of the

A lone hiker heads out on the slick Huckleberry Trail, from its southern trailhead.

old Passenger and Freight Depot (1912) is now occupied by the Blacksburg Municipal Building. Taking off, you pass a picnic area in about half a mile, and find yourself in the realm of Virginia Tech. Cross over South Gate Drive and Country Club Drive. At mile 1.2, at the Tech Center Drive intersection, a trail branch leads to the Virginia Tech Corporate Research Center; at mile 1.4 is the Virginia Tech Seismological Observatory.

Beyond the U.S. 460 bypass (mile 1.8), wetlands edge the trailside, where peepers and bullfrogs croak, an amphibian symphony in spring. Pass Mabry Lane (mile 2.9), Huckleberry Lane (mile 3.2), Hightop Road (mile 3.4), and Merrimac Road (mile 4). At mile 4.3 you come to the Merrimac Mine Tipple Site, with the concrete foundation visible beside the trail. Montgomery County has acquired some thirty acres along both sides of the trail that were previously occupied by the Merrimac Mine and its company town, and has plans to develop a historical park.

At mile 5 you cross a pedestrian bridge over the Norfolk Southern mainline. Stop and look for the three concrete abutments of the old railroad bridge that still stand next to the pedestrian bridge. The mainline is one of two routes used by Norfolk Southern coal trains between the coalfields of Virginia, West Virginia, and Kentucky and the port of Hampton Roads. Sometimes you can see coal trains slowly chugging beneath your feet. To the east rises the western portal of the Merrimac Tunnel. The tunnel burrows beneath the eastern Continental Divide; from the western portal, waters flow to the New River and ultimately to the Gulf of Mexico, while from the eastern portal waters flow to the North Fork Roanoke River and eventually to the Atlantic Ocean.

Farther along, at mile 5.5, awaits the Corning Industrial Rail Spur Crossing. Tips of arrows and spears, stone tools, and other artifacts found beneath the cornfields here have been dated back to 8000 B.C., showing that this area was used by Native Americans as transient hunting and fishing camps. This section of the trail has thus been constructed over geotextile fabric so as not to disturb the subsurface soils and any artifacts located therein.

Proceeding along, you pass more wetlands and wood thickets, and soon you'll see the New River Valley Mall looming atop a green hill.

14 Lake Accotink Trail

This wide dirt trail travels around a forested lake in the heart of suburbia—a not-so-secret escape for evening and weekend jaunts.

Activities: [icons]

Notes: Mountain bike or hybrid preferred.

Location: Lake Accotink Park in Springfield, Fairfax County, just outside the Capital Beltway (I–495)

Length: 3.75 miles round-trip

Surface: Dirt and gravel

Wheelchair access: Yes, although the trail is bumpy and gravelly in places.

Difficulty: Easy. The trail is wide and virtually flat.

Food: There's a snack bar at the park's marina office.

Rest rooms: There's a portable toilet in the lower parking area.

Seasons: Open year-round. The trail can be extremely crowded on warm evenings and weekends. Autumn brings especially beautiful changing foliage.

Access and parking: You can access the trail from two locations:
- *Lake Accotink Park:* Pick up the trail at the marina in Lake Accotink Park. To find it off the Capital Beltway (I–495) in Springfield, take Braddock Road (exit 5) west, heading outside the beltway. Turn left at the second light, onto Queensbury Avenue. Follow this to the end and turn right onto Heming Avenue. The park entrance is a third of a mile farther on the right.
- *Rolling Road:* You can also access the trail at Rolling Road and Danbury Forest Drive in Springfield.

Rentals: Nothing in Springfield but rentals are available nearby in Alexandria and Shirlington:
- Big Wheel Bikes, 2 Prince Street, Alexandria, VA 22314; (703) 739–2300.
- Metropolis Bicycles, 4056 28th Street S., Arlington, VA 22206; (703) 671–1700; located in Shirlington, just off I–395.

Contact: Lake Accotink Park, 5660 Heming Avenue, Springfield, VA 22150; (703) 569–3464.

• •

Close enough to D.C. for a quick spin or stroll after work, the Lake Accotink Trail encircles Lake Accotink, a pretty body of water anchored by an old-fashioned carousel, miniature golf course, and little beach. About half of the trail began as the rail bed for the Orange & Alexandria Railroad.

The O&A was built in the 1840s to haul goods from the port of Alexandria to the farms of Manassas. But then, along came the Civil War, when it suddenly gained strategic military importance. Indeed, on December 27, 1863, Gen. J. E. B. Stuart and his Confederate raiders tore up the railroad track and burned the bridge across Accotink Creek. In postbellum years, the line merged with the Manassas Gap Railroad, which went bankrupt in 1871.

Begin your jaunt by heading west of the marina toward the tall railroad trestle, crossing a small stone bridge behind the dam (you'll have to turn around if the bridge is under water). Follow the path parallel to the still-active railroad trestle and head toward the woods. There's a quick hill to scramble up, and then the trail curves through mature hardwood upland forest, the peaceful domain of gray squirrels, raccoons, and opossums.

As soon as the trail straightens out, you'll know you're on the old train corridor. The lake isn't visible, but the various tones of duck-quacking will assure you that water is not far away. Sporadic wetlands confirm this assumption.

About a mile from the dam, you'll pass by suburban backyards

The still-active CSX railroad trestle lies just beyond Lake Accotink.

(wave to the people eating their breakfast *en plein air*), then come to a sign for the Lake Accotink Park Trail, pointing to the walkway to the right. Ignore it for now, following the old rail bed for another 1.5 wooded miles to Rolling Road; the last mile doubles as a service road for a power substation.

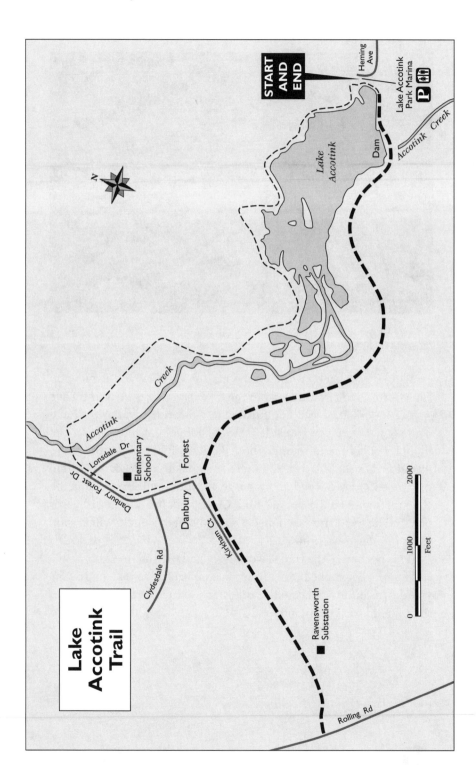

Lake Accotink Trail

START AND END

Heming Ave

Lake Accotink Park Marina

P

Accotink Creek

Dam

Lake Accotink

N

Accotink Creek

Lonsdale Dr

Danbury Forest Dr

Elementary School

Danbury Forest

Clydesdale Rd

Kirkham Ct

Ravensworth Substation

Rolling Rd

0   1000   2000

Feet

Canada Geese are ever-present icons along the Lake Accolink Trail, here near the marina.

Rather than backtracking to the marina the way you came, you can continue to circumnavigate the lake by going back to the Lake Accotink Park Trail sign and turning left, down the walkway. You'll come out at Danbury Forest Drive; walk straight ahead, past an elementary school, and reenter the Lake Accotink Trail on the right, just after Lonsdale Drive. Concrete steps take you back down into the woods. Cross a wooden bridge, go 40 yards, and turn right at the trail junction. You'll cross Accotink Creek and, in another 120 yards or so, come to a T intersection. Go right, along the creek, which soon spills into Lake Accotink.

This portion of the trail is woodsy, edged with some unobtrusive residences. As you near the marina, a couple of short side paths take you down to the water's edge, offering good views of the lake and the railroad trestle beyond.

Following one of the world's oldest rivers, the spectacular New River Trail—a linear state park—explores an especially remote corner of Virginia, where the river and forest and historical mining tidbits are your constant companions.

Activities:

Notes: Mountain bikes or hybrids required. If you wish to only ride point-to-point, Virginia Heights Bicycle Shop (540–228–8311) has a shuttle that will drop you off at the beginning or pick you up at the end.

Location: From Galax to Dora Junction, with a spur to Fries, in Grayson, Carroll, Wythe, and Pulaski Counties of southwestern Virginia

Length: 57 miles one-way

Surface: Cinder and ballast stone

Wheelchair access: Yes

Difficulty: Moderate

Food: Generally the trail is remote; it is advisable to pack your own food to bring with you. You'll find groceries and/or food at the following stops: Pulaski (northern trailhead), Draper (mile 6.2), Foster Falls campground (mile 24), Fries (mile 44.5), Cliffview (mile 49.5), and Galax (mile 51.8).

Rest rooms: The following sites have portable or flush toilets: Pulaski (northern trailhead), Shot Tower State Historical Park (mile 25.3), Fries (mile 44.5), Cliffview (mile 49.5), and Galax (mile 51.8).

Seasons: Open year-round. The peak months are April through June, and September through November. Summers in the New River Valley are hot and humid, and sudden releases of water can occur from dams.

Access and parking: The major access points, with parking, are:

- *Pulaski* (northern trailhead): From I–81 take VA–99 west about 2 miles to Xaloy; turn onto Xaloy and drive to entrance.
- *Draper* (mile 6.2): From I–81 take Route 658 east through Draper. Parking is available across from Brysons Grocery Store, less than a mile from the interstate.
- *Shot Tower State Historical Park* (mile 25.3): From I–77 (exit 24), go east on Route 69 to VA–52, and follow signs to Shot Tower.

- *Cliffview* (mile 49.5): From I-77, take U.S. 58/211 west to Galax; proceed north on Route 887 to Cliffview Road (Route 721), and go left. The parking area is on the left, across from Cliffview Mansion and the Cliffview Trading Post.
- *Galax* (mile 51.8): From I-77, follow U.S. 58/211 west to Galax; parking and trail access where U.S. 58 crosses Chestnut Creek, just before you enter downtown.

The New River Trail can also be accessed at Hiwassee, Allisonia, Austinville, Ivanhoe, Lone Ash, Barren Springs, and Fries, but there is no developed parking at these entrances.

For horses, there is parking at Cliffview, Shot Tower State Historical Park, and Draper.

Rentals: Rentals are available nearby:
- Tangent Outfitters, c/o Java River Co., 1055 Norwood Street, Bradford, VA 24141; (540) 674-5202.
- Virginia Heights Bicycle Shop, 1007 North Fourth Street, Wytheville, VA 24382; (540) 228-8311.

Contact: New River Trail State Park, Route 1, Box 81X, Austinville, VA 24312; (540) 699-6778.

• •

Traversing the luxuriant highlands of southwestern Virginia, the New River Trail spends a good amount of time hugging the New River, which, paradoxically, is a waterway that is older than the mountains it crosses, perhaps the oldest river in North America. Spectacular cliffs, where the ancient river has cut through rock, highlight pristine views, while abundant wildlife forages on the riverbanks. Along the way, remnants of old mining towns dot the trailside, providing a touch of history to a beautiful, remote landscape.

You will be following the old route of the Cripple Creek Branch of the Norfolk & Western Railway (N&W), first constructed in the early 1880s to serve the area's blossoming mining operations. N&W's officials believed that Wythe County held the largest, most diverse supply of quality minerals in the United States. Numerous boomtowns sprang up around railroad stops along the way, many of whose ruins you can still see today. Through the years, the railroad carried iron, lead, and zinc, in addition to timber, livestock, furniture, and passengers. Be sure to look at the cinders spread along the trail bed, remnants

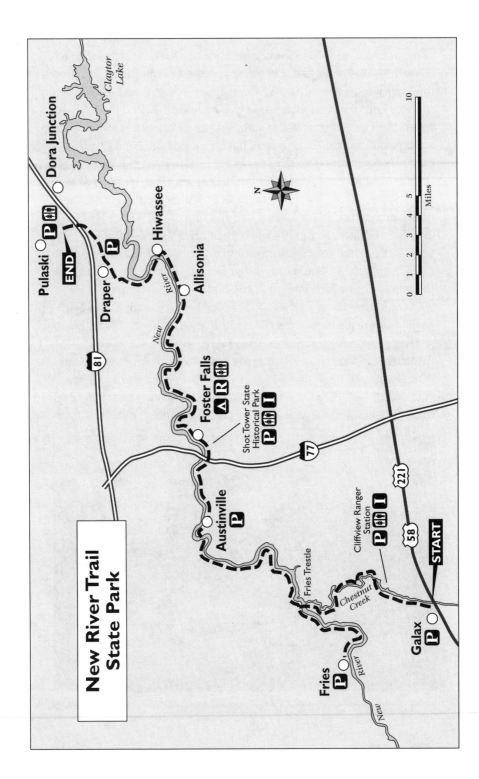

New River Trail State Park

of burnt coal used to power steam locomotives that once rolled through these hills and valleys. In another hundred years, the mining industry dwindled, and the last train ran in October 1985. A few months later the Norfolk Southern (which then owned the line) donated the right-of-way to the state for the development of a linear state park. Outdoor enthusiasts have enjoyed the New River Trail ever since.

The New River Trail runs from milepost 2 at Dora Junction (where the Cripple Creek Branch joined the mainline) to Galax, with a 5-mile spur leading to Fries. Keep in mind that the trail from Hiwassee Trestle to Galax runs uphill—not a huge uphill, but definitely up. As such, people like to start from Fries or Galax, and ride downhill to Draper or Pulaski. You can arrange for a shuttle to drop you off at the beginning or pick you up at the end.

This journey begins in Galax, at mile 51.8. Originally called Bonaparte, the town's name was changed in 1904 in honor of the heart-shaped galax leaf that grows abundantly in the area (and was the first cargo shipped from town on the new N&W line). But what Galax is really known for is its fiddling. Come the second weekend in August, you'll be treated to the Old Fiddlers' Convention, where daytime farmers and factory workers, businessmen and small-town

Hiwassee Bridge remains one of the most photographed spots along the New River Trail.

shopkeepers come together to twang the night away.

To find the Galax Branch trail from I–77, follow U.S. 58/221 west to Galax. The trailhead is at the U.S. 58 bridge over Chestnut Creek, just before downtown. There's a parking area on the right side of the road. Leaving Galax, the trail—rather rugged at first, with chunky pieces of gravel—follows pretty Chestnut Creek through hillscapes and farmland. At mile 49.5 lies the community of Cliffview, where a ranger station offers rest rooms and drinking water. Look to the trail's west side for Cliffside Manor, once home to Thomas L. Felts, a state senator and the owner of the Baldwin-Felts Detective Agency. His mine guards protected the coal companies of central Appalachia and Colorado during the violent labor struggles in the early 1900s.

Ahead is a cement cairn marked P48, measuring the number of miles from here to Pulaski. About a mile farther, Iron Mines Junction is an open iron ore pit and shaft. Just exactly what all this mining does to the landscape is apparent about half a mile farther, where a small creek from the iron-mining watershed spills into Chestnut Creek. All the surrounding trees and plants are dead, victims of the high acidity level.

At mile 40.6 you enter the curved, 195-foot-long Chestnut Tunnel, its dark, rough-cut interior giving it a cavelike appearance. Check out the timbers and boards supporting its north end. Within less than a mile, rapid-filled Chestnut Creek becomes slow and deep, and you come to 1,059-foot-long Fries Trestle, the longest bridge span on the trail. This is where you first meet up with the New River; note its unusual south-to-north flow.

At the end of the bridge, the 5-mile Fries Branch trail goes left, paralleling the New River the entire way. Some of the best river views are found along this length, as well as some of the best chances to survey the effects of beaver activity. Around mile 41.5 especially, trees along the river bear the indicative gashed, pointed stumps left by busy beavers. You approach town about 3.5 miles farther on. Begun as a cotton mill company town in the early 1900s, Fries (pronounced "freeze") still boasts some of its frame houses built for mill employees. In town, an original N&W caboose now serves as the town information center.

Back at the Fries Trestle, the main trail proceeds northeast, past a handful of picnic tables and a shade shelter. Brace yourself for the breathtaking views that lie ahead, with wooded mountain slopes rising to the left, the broad river flowing on the right between grassy banks and mudflats. In spring, dogwood and pink wild cherry add splashes of color to the scene. At mile 38.6 you reach Byllesby Dam, completed in 1913 by Appalachian Power. It was the first of its kind for the power company, earning it the reputation as a prominent electrical power producer. Its cool blue waters now cover the site of Grayson Sulphur Springs, a popular health resort in operation from 1835 to 1913 (except for a spell during the Civil War). Residents and visitors alike basked in the rugged mountain beauty, and sought to cure their ailments in the spring waters. Byllesby was a passenger stop on the railroad until 1951; the last railroad station, a little frame structure, still stands next to the brick building at the dam's entrance.

About 3 miles ahead you get a good view of "Lake Buck" and Buck Dam, also completed by Appalachian Power in the early 1900s. Near the spillway, the Cliff Trail follows an old wagon road parallel to the New River Trail, rejoining the latter at Ivanhoe.

This tunnel can be found along the trail in the town of Austinville, once the heart of the area's mining operations.

You pass through the town of Ivanhoe at mile 32.8, once the site of a number of lead mines and iron furnaces, then cross the Ivanhoe Bridge, featuring exceptional stonework. Big Branch enters the New River at this point, its clear waters mingling with the New's muddy.

More mining history awaits at Austinville, where mines began operating in 1756, providing most of the lead for the Revolutionary War and for the Confederacy in the Civil War. The railroad was lured to the area specifically for this town's mining importance. When they

The Foster Falls Depot, perched right next to the trail, is a leftover from the days of a once-bustling mining community.

closed in 1981, the Austinville mines were the oldest continuously running mining operation in the United States. Beyond mile marker 30, remnants of these industries dot the trailside, including the shafts' elevator buildings. At mile 27.7 you pass a white farmhouse; some believe the log cabin behind it was the birthplace of Stephen F. Austin, the father of Texas. His father, Moses Austin, owned the local mines and, in fact, Austinville bears his name.

Nearing Shot Tower State Historical Park, the trail's midpoint, the trail becomes smoother and especially pretty, with steep outcrops rising to one side, the soul-nourishing river on the other. Truly breathtaking. At Shot Tower (mile 25.3), a 75-foot-tall tower built about 1807 atop a grassy knoll, you can learn how molten lead poured through a sieve at the top of the tower was dropped down its hollow interior to make ammunition.

Beyond Shot Tower, the trail continues to embrace the river's north bank, with steep rock walls crowding the trail's south side. At mile 24 you come to Foster Falls, the name given to both the rushing torrent of rapids on the New River and to the settlement here. The iron furnace here processed up to 2,000 tons of pig iron a year.

The most visible remains of the once-bustling community are the Foster Falls Depot, perched right next to the trail, and the Foster Falls Hotel, just off the trail, which operated until 1919. There is a state-operated campground here, complete with bike rentals, food, and rest rooms.

Just up the way (mile 22.7) awaits a curious relic from railroading days; look for the old wooden steps leading to a stone arch. When the N&W built this section of line, they constructed over a spring-house, allowing a local farmer to keep his only means of refrigeration in the days before electricity.

Proceeding along, at mile 20.1 you pass the Calfee Cemetery, the century-old burial grounds of a local influential landowning family. Look for Bertha Cave (mile 19.6), formed in the surrounding limestone rock and supposedly full of bats. At mile 17.4 you come to the Barren Springs Furnace, originally built in 1853 and rebuilt in 1873. Once standing 40 feet high and producing five to six tons of pig iron a day, its ruins resemble a large rock formation tangled with vegetation.

Onward you pass beneath VA–100, beyond which the river views open wide, to the left. Cross into Pulaski County (marked by a stone marker) and, at mile 14.1, pass by an old ore washer, used by a local mining operation to separate the metal from ore. It's the low stone wall halfway up the hillside.

After another mile, you pass a spur line, one of many branches that forked from the main trail to access mines. This one was called the Betty Baker Line, which followed pretty Little Reed Island Creek to an iron ore strip mine back in the hills.

Continue along the trail, fragrant in spring with blooming blackberries and multiflora roses. At mile 12.5 you cross a bridge into the community of Allisonia. Established in 1872 and named for an early pioneer family, the charming town once housed the headquarters of five mining operations. Stroll the streets to admire the turn-of-the-century architecture, including a Baptist church built in 1891. The Allisonia Depot and a railroad station foreman's house still stand on the trail's river side.

Next you come to the stunning Hiwassee Trestle, measuring 951 feet long. Hiwassee once was another flourishing mining community, known for its vividly colored ocher, umber, and sienna ores—300 different shades of pigment! Since the 1920s, the Hoover Color Corporation has shipped these nontoxic pigments throughout the United States and, indeed, the world, and is the only remaining mining operation in Pulaski County.

Now begins an uphill climb all the way to Draper. At Delton Trestle (mile 8), the trail leaves the New River, entering a bucolic landscape of rolling fields. Draper, at mile 6.2, has a bit of interesting architecture, especially the Draper Mercantile, which still houses the post office, and Brysons Grocery Store, purveyors of ice cream, chips, and other trail necessities. Both date from circa 1882 and once formed the center of town activity.

Descending into the Pulaski area, you pass by the McAdam whistle stop (mile 3.8), a railroad stop that had no depot or station. Another relic of the past, the railroad crossing signal at mile 2.6 is the only original signal on the entire trail. Farther along, a railroad sign with a W indicates another whistle stop.

The trail currently ends at Dora Junction, at mile marker 2, 1 mile shy of Pulaski.

A runner crosses the Dalton Bridge near Galax.

Beginning atop Whitetop Mountain, this spellbinding trail zips down the wild mountainside, over wooded canyons, beside fish-filled streams, to its midway point at Damascus. Beyond town, the scenery calms, taking in chocolate-box views of barn dotted fields, fat cows, and wide, lazy rivers. The best tactic to ride this trail is to take a shuttle from Abingdon or Damascus to the mountaintop, then enjoy the descent.

Activities:

Notes: Biking this trail requires a mountain bike or hybrid. Camping is permitted on national forest land only.

Location: Abingdon to the Virginia–North Carolina border (1.1 miles east of Whitetop Station, Virginia), in Washington and Grayson Counties of southwestern Virginia

Length: 34.3 miles one-way

Surface: Cinder and crushed stone, manageable even after heavy downpours. At worst the footing is sandy.

Wheelchair access: Wheelchairs with large tires can travel downhill from Creek Junction to Damascus.

Difficulty: It depends on which way you're traveling. Difficult, if you start the trail at Abingdon or Damascus and ride up the mountain. Moderate, if you shuttle to Whitetop and enjoy the ride down.

Food: Abingdon and Damascus have restaurants and groceries. It's recommended to take water and snacks with you.

Rest rooms: Portable toilets or rest rooms at Whitetop Station (mile 33.4), Green Cove Station (mile 30.2), Taylors Valley (mile 21.9), and Damascus (mile 16.4).

Seasons: Open year-round. Spring is absolutely stunning, with the suite of budding wildflowers. Be prepared for the crowds on warm summer weekends. Winter can bring ice and snow.

Access and parking: The main access points, with parking areas, are:
- *Whitetop Station* (mile 33.2): From Abingdon go south for more than 20 miles on U.S. 58 to Route 755; go right for 2 miles.

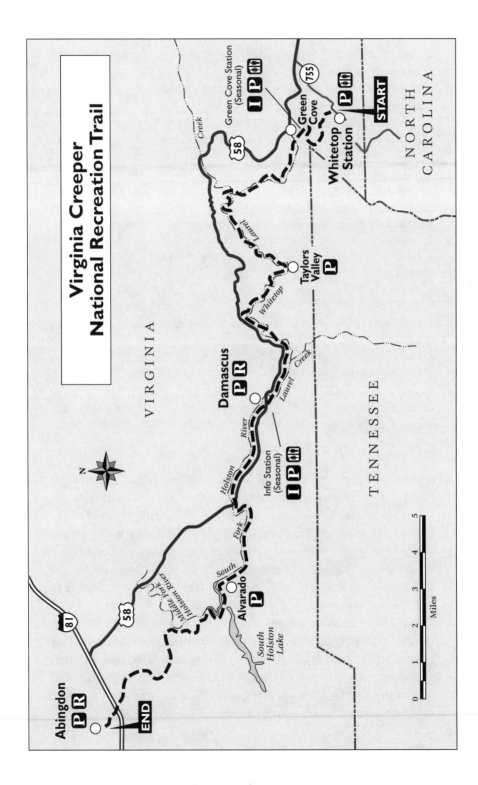

- *Green Cove* (mile 30.2): From Abingdon, go south on U.S. 58 to Route 600 and go right.
- *Taylors Valley* (mile 21.9): From Damascus, go south on VA–91; 1 mile south of the Tennessee state line, turn left on Route 725.
- *Damascus* (mile 16.4): Go south of Abingdon on U.S. 58.
- *Alvarado* (mile 9.4): From Abingdon go south 5 miles on U.S. 58 to Route 722; go right to Route 710 and park along the road.
- *Abingdon* (mile 0): From Main Street, go south on Pecan Street to the trail-head near the corner of A Street, S.E., and Green Springs Road.

There are also several street crossings where roadside parking is available.

Rentals and shuttle services: Several companies rent bikes, as well as offer shuttle services up Whitetop from Abingdon or Damascus:

- Adventure Damascus, 128 Laurel Avenue, Damascus, VA 24236; (540) 475–6262.
- Blue Blaze Bike & Shuttle, 227 Laurel Avenue, Damascus, VA 24236; (800) 475–5095.
- Highland Bike Rental, 302 Green Spring Road, Abingdon, VA 24210; (540) 628–9672.
- Mount Rogers Outfitters, 110 Laurel Avenue, Damascus, VA 24236; (540) 475–5416 or (877) 475–5416.

Contact: Mount Rogers National Recreation Area, Route 1, Box 303, Marion, VA 24354; (540) 783–5196. Abingdon Convention & Visitors Bureau, 335 Cummings Street, Abingdon, VA 24210; (540) 676–2282 or (800) 435–3440.

• • • • • • • • • • • • • • • • • • • •

The Creeper may very well be the prettiest trail in this book. It certainly is on a sunny spring day, when you have nothing to do but sail down Whitetop Mountain, taking in dramatic views of misty blue mountains, plush pastures dotted with Wyethesque barns, green-and-yellow fields, boulder-strewn mountain streams, and deep forested canyons. This is not a rail-trail exclusively beloved by locals, although locals must eternally be grateful for its proximity. Rather, it is a destination, one that you should go out of your way for.

This piece of heaven began as the Virginia-Carolina Railroad, a true mountain railroad built in the early 1900s between Abingdon and Elkland, North Carolina, to haul trees off Whitetop Mountain and surrounding peaks. In 1918 the Norfolk & Western Railroad bought the line, heralding the railroad's glory days. Up to eight trains ran a day, carrying lumber, iron ore, supplies, and passengers. Even in its day, the railroad was recognized for its beautiful and rugged terrain; indeed, the 16.8-mile section from Damascus to Whitetop mounts a one-way elevation gain of 1,646 feet. Imagine the task of railroad crews, responsible for keeping the trains running across more than one hundred trestles and bridges, through endless rock slides and washouts.

It was economics that finally did the railroad in. The Great Depression coincided with the exhaustion of most of the area's timber, and traffic nose-dived. The West Jefferson to Elkland and the Creek Junction to Konnarock sections were the first to go, in 1933. The rest of the Abingdon Branch from Abingdon to West Jefferson limped on as a sleepy rural line, living up to its nickname, the Virginia Creeper. The last train ran on March 31, 1977. The N&W sold the abandoned right-of-way in the 1980s to the towns of Abingdon and Damascus and to the National Forest Service, which worked together to convert it into the spectacular recreational trail it is today. In 1987 Congress declared it a national recreation trail.

The Virginia Creeper really has two different moods: Wild mountain terrain, with its spitting rivers and steep crevasses, highlights the 16-odd miles between Whitetop Station and Damascus, while the 16.8-mile section from Damascus to Abingdon is much more peaceful, traversing rolling farmland dotted with cows and crisscrossed with wide, lazy streams. The most popular way to tackle the trail is by shuttle from either Abingdon or Damascus. You get a lift to the top of Whitetop, with nothing to do but zoom back down. The most spectacular segment is, no doubt, between Whitetop Junction and Damascus, so if time is limited make sure to plan accordingly.

A note on mileages: The mileages in this narrative are listed according to

Water rushes over the rocks in Whitetop Laurel Creek on the Virginia Creeper Trail.

new mile markers set along the trail, which begin at the trailhead in Abingdon at mile 0 and end at the North Carolina state line at mile 34.3. Ignore the original cement markers, which were positioned in reference to their distance from the Abingdon train station, about half a mile farther than the trailhead.

The highest point on the trail (3,576 feet) is on Whitetop Mountain at Whitetop Station (mile 33.4), once the highest passenger station east of the Rockies and a booming lumber community in the early 1900s. This is where your adventure begins. To reach it from I-81 (or Abingdon), go south on U.S. 58 for more than 20 miles; turn right on Route 726 and follow signs to Whitetop Station. Better yet, as suggested above, take a shuttle from Abingdon or Damascus, so you don't need to retrieve your car after a long day of riding.

At the Whitetop Station trailhead, you can turn right and follow the rough and isolated trail to its terminus (mile 34.3), at the Virginia–North Carolina border. Most people don't do this, however, because you just have to turn back again and, as Jim of the Blue Blaze shuttle service says, the only things in that direction are a beaver dam and the original cast of *Deliverance*.

The Virginia Creeper has 75 trestles. This one is located near the town of Damascus.

Turning left on the trail at Whitetop Station will please you more. Tunneling through shadowy woods, the 3 miles between Whitetop and Green Cove offer the steepest downhills (meaning very little pedaling!). Be careful as you negotiate occasional washouts and really gravely sections. Where virgin forest once stood, second-growth (yellow poplar, red maple, eastern hemlock, eastern red cedar, white pine, black cherry, black locust, yellow birch) now thrives; in spring you'll see the pale pink blooms of apple trees, descendants of apple seeds and cores once tossed from the trains. In a little more than a mile stands an original railroad marker labeled A33, indicating the number of miles from here to the old Abingdon train station. Soon after, you're lifted high above the forest floor on your first trestle, one of more than seventy-five along the way.

CREEPING ALONG

The Abingdon Branch became known as the Virginia Creeper in the 1930s and '40s, although exactly where, how, and why no one knows for sure. Maybe the track's curvaceous course reminded people of the ubiquitous native vine called Virginia creeper. Or perhaps it's because the train had to negotiate such sharp curves and steep grades, and so it could only slowly creep up and down the mountain.

Now and again the woods open up, taking in wide swaths of sky-scraping mountains and velvety green pastures, the epitome of Blue Ridge highlands beauty. At mile 30.3 you enter the town of Green Cove, snuggled in a lovely farmscape. Here you'll see one of many Christmas tree farms that flank the mountainside, along with the only train depot left standing on the entire route. Resurrected as a little museum preserving both store goods (the building was also once a pharmacy and post office) and railroad memorabilia, the little green-and-white structure is open on summer weekends.

Beyond town you join the Green Cove Creek, its banks embellished in late June and early July with blooming rhododendrons. All along the way, the creek's cool waters beckon you to shaded shores, a perfect excuse to take a break. Among the many wooden trestles you glide across is the trail's highest, at Creek Junction (mile 27).

Fittingly named High Trestle, it measures 550 feet long and 100 feet tall, offering supreme views of the surrounding mountainscape. The famed Appalachian Trail joins you across the trestle, and for a little distance beyond.

The trail soon sidles beside Whitetop Laurel Creek as it tumbles through a forested gorge—stupendous scenery, indeed. This is quite possibly the finest trout stream in Virginia, with both rainbow and brownies. The number of anglers lining its banks will testify. At mile 23 you visit the hamlet of Taylors Valley, with a picnic area and portable toilet. At one point you pass through someone's front yard, marked off by gates . . . kind of odd. Leaving Taylors Valley, the Whitetop enters another gorge, its churning white waters washing jagged rocks. At mile 19 the trail parallels U.S. 58, signaling that you're about 2 miles from Damascus. You cross a couple more trestles, including a great iron one, and soon enter town (mile 16.8), a major supply point along the Appalachian Trail; say hi to the people as you pass by their backyards. The community park here has rest rooms, drinking water, picnic tables, vending machines, a diminutive steam locomotive that's fun to climb on, and an old caboose that now serves as a trail information center.

Beyond Damascus, the trail continues to parallel U.S. 58 for about 2 miles, then passes beneath it and leaves it behind. Soon the Creeper takes on a gentler character, as it follows Laurel Creek through sunny pastures dotted with cows. The trail can be a bit bumpy in this section. At mile 14 you pass the only place where the original tracks remain, par-

tially buried beneath asphalt. By mile 13 you are following the South Fork Holston River, one of the best flyfishing streams in the Southeast.

At mile 12 comes the first in a series of gates along this section, basically erected

The quaint Green Cove depot at mile 30.2 is the only train depot left standing on the Virginia Creeper Trail.

to keep the cows in. Although the public has the legal right to use the trail, much of the land in this section is privately owned. Please be sure to stay on the trail, and to close the gates along the way. Pass through Alvarado at mile 8.9, site of an old station, then, in just over another mile, cross the wooden, curved, 529-foot-long South Holston Trestle. Here, stop and look northeast toward Damascus, where you can see the confluence of the Middle and South Forks of the Holston River. Refusing at first to mingle, the two flow side by side, the Middle running muddy and the South clear. Finally they give in, mixing beneath your feet. This is the lowest point on the trail, 1,900 feet above sea level. (That means you're in for a bit of uphill—just a 1.3 percent grade)

Now you travel through an area called the River Knobs (rapids filled with cobbles, rock gardens, and tiny ledges), following the noisy Middle Fork Holston in the shadow of 300-foot-high hills. A pandemonium of wildflowers decorates the trail in spring, including bloodroot, spring beauty, bellwort, Solomon's seal, and foamflower. In summer, blue Virginia dayflower, stonecrop, and pipsissewa take over, while late summer brings purple ironweed and pink joe-pye weed. Around mile 7 you cut through an alley of moss-covered rocks, seemingly more Irish than American. Then, just before mile marker 6 awaits a postcard-perfect farmscape, its bright red barn contrasting perfectly against spring's blanket of flowers on surrounding hills. Another barn awaits at mile 4.4, a venerable beauty nearly toppled over.

You pass by the site of the old Watauga station at mile 3.9, crossing over another wonderful old trestle, then slither above serpentine Berry Creek, crisscrossed with beaver dams. Around mile 2.8 you enter an area called the Great Knobs, after a series of ridges that run parallel to Holston and Iron Mountains to the southeast.

Before you know it, the trail passes through the Glenrochie Country Club golf course, ducks under I–81 (mile 0.8), crosses Town Creek on the last trestle, and enters the town of Abingdon, America's first incorporated town west of the Blue Ridge and now ranked as one of America's 100 top art towns. You know you've reached the end when you spy one of the line's original steam locomotives perched at the trailhead.

Beginning amid the capital's suburban sprawl, the ever popular W&OD Trail heads west through Virginia's fabled green countryside, sprinkled with horse farms, pastures, little towns, and burbling creeks.

Activities:

Notes: The crushed stone equestrian path parallels the paved bike path from west of Vienna (mile 12) to Purcellville (mile 45.5).

Location: Between Arlington and Purcellville, in Arlington, Fairfax, and Loudoun Counties of northern Virginia

Length: 45.5 miles one-way

Surface: Asphalt

Wheelchair access: Yes. The trail is smooth and, at worst, rolling.

Difficulty: Easy. The trail is rolling in places, but nothing too strenuous.

Food: There are lots of opportunities for food along the way. The main stops for groceries and restaurants include Shirlington (trailhead), Falls Church (mile 7), Vienna (mile 12), Reston (mile 18), Herndon (mile 20), Leesburg (miles 33–35), and Purcellville (mile 45.5).

Rest rooms: Portable toilets or rest rooms are available at Bluemont Park in Arlington (mile 3.5, Wilson Boulevard), Vienna Community Center (mile 11.6), Herndon Community Center (mile 20.5), Ashburn (mile 27.7, at Ashburn Road), and Catoctin Circle in Leesburg (mile 33.8).

Seasons: Open year-round. Warm weather brings trail users out of the woodwork. Remember that summer's sun can be relentless, especially in the largely treeless stretch between Herndon and Leesburg. A water bottle is absolutely necessary if you're determined to undertake this leg.

Access and parking: Available at street crossings all along the trail, and at the following locations:

- *Arlington/Shirlington* (mile 0): Take I–395 to the Shirlington exit (exit 6), bear to the right, heading north on Shirlington Road. Turn left on South Four Mile Run Drive; the W&OD Trail will be on the right paralleling the road. You can park along the side of the road. Don't leave your car overnight.
- *East Falls Church metro:* From I–66 east, take the Sycamore Street exit.

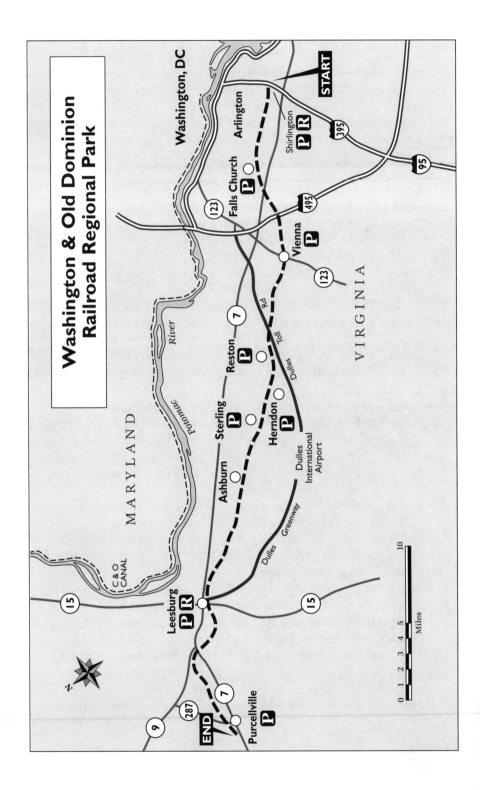

Washington & Old Dominion
Railroad Regional Park

Washington, DC

MARYLAND

Potomac River

C & O CANAL

VIRGINIA

Arlington

Shirlington

Falls Church

Vienna

Reston

Sterling

Ashburn

Herndon

Dulles Toll Rd

Dulles International Airport

Dulles Greenway

Leesburg

Purcellville

START

END

395

95

495

123

123

7

15

15

7

287

9

N

0 1 2 3 4 5   10
Miles

Turn right on Sycamore, left on Washington Boulevard, and then left into the metro parking lot. Weekend parking only.

- *Dunn Loring:* Take I-495 to the Gallows Road/U.S. 50 exit and follow signs toward Gallows Road north; turn right on Gallows. Go past the trail, turn right on Idylwood Road, and right on Sandburg Street. There are gravel lots on both sides of the road at the trail.
- *Vienna East:* From Tysons Corner take Chain Bridge Road/VA-123 into Vienna. Turn left on Park Street, then right into the Vienna Community Center parking lot. The trail runs between the parking lot and the center.
- *Vienna West:* From Tysons Corner take Chain Bridge Road/VA-123 into Vienna, turn right on Park Street, left at a four-way stop sign onto Church Street, right onto Mill Street, left onto Ayr Hill Avenue, and then left into the gravel parking lot at the train station.
- *Reston:* From Tysons Corner take VA-7 west, then turn left onto the Reston Parkway. Turn left onto Sunset Hills Road, then left onto Old Reston Avenue. There is a paved parking lot on the right by the trail. There is also a large commuter parking lot next to the trail farther down Sunset Hills Road, although it is typically full on weekdays. However, if you are coming from the Dulles toll road, take the Reston Parkway exit, go right on Sunset Hills Road, and left on Old Reston Avenue to the paved parking lot.
- *Herndon:* From the Dulles toll road, take the Centreville Road exit, and go right. Centreville Road becomes Elden Street. Turn left on Station Street, and go to the large town municipal center parking lot at the end.
- *Sterling/VA-28:* From the Dulles toll road, take Sully Road/VA-28 north. Several miles north of the Dulles Airport, watch for W&OD parking signs. There is a large lot, good for horse trailers.
- *Leesburg:* Take the Dulles Greenway to Leesburg. At the Leesburg Bypass (U.S. 15/VA-7), go north to the VA-7 exit. Head east to Sycolin Street, and turn immediately right into the parking lot for the Douglass Community Center, parking at the rear of the building. The trail is directly behind the building through the picnic area.
- *Leesburg West:* Take the Dulles Greenway to Leesburg. At the Leesburg Bypass (U.S. 15/VA-7), go north to the VA-7 exit. Head east, past Sycolin Street, to Catoctin Circle. Go left. There is a gravel parking lot on the left, right at the trail crossing. Or, continue on Catoctin Circle to Dry Mill Road. Here, turn immediately right into the parking lot of Loudoun County High School (for parking on weekends only during the school year). The trail is several hundred yards farther down Catoctin Circle.
- *Purcellville:* Take VA-7 west from Leesburg. Exit at VA-287 and turn left;

at Hirst Road turn right, then turn left on Maple Street. Turn left into the parking lot of Loudoun Valley High School. Weekend parking only during the school year.

- *Purcellville West:* Take VA–7 west from Leesburg. Exit at VA–287 and go south to Purcellville. Turn right onto Business VA–7, right onto Hatcher Street, and right again into the gravel parking lot at the trail.

Rentals: Rentals are available nearby:

- Bicycle Outfitters, 19 Catoctin Circle N.E., Leesburg, VA 20176; (703) 777–6126.
- Metropolis Bicycles, 4056 28th Street S., Arlington, VA 22206; (703) 671–1700.

Contact: Northern Virginia Regional Park Authority, 5400 Ox Road, Fairfax Station, VA 22039; (703) 352–5900.

• •

Beloved by commuters and weekend escapees alike, the Washington & Old Dominion Trail snakes from the shores of the Potomac through classic Virginia countryside, stopping just short of the misty Blue Ridge. Along the way it visits an eclectic mix of sights: sweet little hamlets, relics of bygone days (including a train museum), a rose garden, an award-winning model town.

This trail is one of the most heavily used rail-trails in the nation. A vast majority of users are from the surrounding communities, many of whom use it daily to run, walk, skate, push baby strollers, ride horses. Still, there's something magical about being able to flee into hillscapes within a stone's throw of one's own home. The scenery gets progressively more pastoral the farther west you go, exceedingly so beyond the Capital Beltway, where the street crossings also become fewer. In my opinion, you can't beat the 10-mile jaunt from the colonial town of Leesburg, at mile 34.5, to the trail's terminus in quaint Purcellville. In no time you escape into luscious farmland, where the midsummer air is sweetened with the scent of ripe blackberries, pungent honeysuckle, and fresh-cut hay. A pure delight.

Starting in 1858, the Washington & Old Dominion Railroad trains chugged along this pretty route (called the Alexandria, Loudoun & Hampshire back then). There were dreams of bringing coal and other riches from the Appalachians to the Potomac, of competing with the powerful Baltimore & Ohio, but the Civil War smudged them out. Never getting any farther than western Loudoun County, the W&OD

LEESBURG: A CITY
WITH A PAST

Forming the heart of charming historic Leesburg, late Georgian and Federal structures cluster around a stately old brick courthouse. A number of these old buildings testify to the town's elegant past. The James Madisons lived at stately Oak Hill, where the president wrote the Monroe Doctrine in 1823, while Gen. George C. Marshall resided at the elegant Dodona Manor. Morven Park, just west of town, is an expansive horse farm centered around a beautiful Greek Revival house. Oatlands, a palatial 1803 mansion with formal gardens, is located 6 miles south of town on U.S. 15.

Leesburg began in 1758 as a trading center, and played a role in many of the nation's formative battles. It was a staging ground for the British during the French and Indian War, and for the Colonials during the Revolutionary War. During the War of 1812, James and Dolley Madison sought refuge from invading British here, allegedly stashing official copies of the Declaration of Independence and the Constitution somewhere nearby. And during the Civil War, Robert E. Lee stopped by on his way to Antietam.

Today it's fun to stroll these ancient, shaded streets, poking into the shops and restaurants now residing within centuries-old walls. You'll find all kinds of wares, ranging from colonial crafts to New Age paraphernalia. My favorite shop: Classy Cat. Housed in an 1820 edifice, it purveys all kinds of cat goodies.

To reach the historic district from the W&OD at mile 34.5, follow King Street (U.S. 15) just a few blocks north. For more information, stop by the Loudoun Tourism Council Visitor Center at Market Station, on the corners of Loudoun and Church Streets (from King Street turn right on Loudoun Street and go one block).

hit its stride in the second and third decades of the twentieth century, at one point running up to forty lines a day to accommodate passengers and freight. But gradually it lost out to cars and buses. Passenger service wound down in 1951, with freight service creeping along the wobbly single track until 1968, its tiny diesels barely reaching speeds of 15 miles an hour. The Virginia Electric and Power

Company bought the abandoned right-of-way in 1972; the Northern Virginia Regional Park purchased it ten years later, after a long, drawn-out deal-making process. Today, the rail-trail is such a fixture of the local community that one wonders what we did before it came along.

The trail officially starts at South Four Mile Run Drive and Shirlington Road in Arlington, just north of Shirlington Village, where this narrative begins. You take off beside rock-strewn Four Mile Run, passing through an unexciting mix of development and small community parks, with plenty of trees to give a semblance of escape. Cross a series of busy roads, including Columbia Pike (mile 1.7), Arlington Boulevard (mile 2.8), and Wilson Boulevard (mile 3.5). At Wilson awaits Bluemont Park, a good rest stop with rest rooms, picnic tables, and a water fountain. Across the street, Bon Air Memorial Rose Garden bursts into a frenzy of sweet-scented blooms June through September.

Safe in a woodsy haven behind a noise wall, you parallel I–66 a bit, then wind through a local park. Follow signs up Tuckahoe Street, skirting the East Falls Church metro station, a popular place to park on weekends. The trail shoots through a perfunctory stretch, crossing several neighborhood streets, to the historic city of Falls Church (mile 7). George Washington and George Mason once were vestrymen at the town's namesake, the extant Falls Church. The only glimpse of the town you get, though, is purely modern-day residential. A bridge sweeps you above car-choked Broad Street (VA–7). A far cry from its nineteenth-century days as a stagecoach route linking Alexandria and Leesburg, today it will lead you to nearby fast-food joints, restaurants, and grocery stores.

Use caution in crossing busy Shreve Road, about half a

Bikers take a much-needed break along the Washington & Old Dominion Railroad trail.

mile beyond the Broad Street overpass. At mile 9 the trail cuts over the Capital Beltway (I–495) and begins to shed its suburban look for something more country. The houses are still around, but the cars are fewer and the woods thicker.

Around mile 11 you come to the town of Vienna, with a number of road crossings. This is a fun place to browse antique shops, eat brunch, stroll the shady streets. History buffs might like to know that the first tactical use of a train in military conflict took place on this section of the railroad, on June 13, 1861. Look for the commemoration plaque beside the trail on Park Street (mile 11.6), near the community center.

At the next street, Maple Avenue, you must cross at one of the stoplights north or south of the trail. Where the trail crosses Church Street (mile 11.9), the nineteenth-century Freeman House stands on the right. A military hospital during the Civil War, this stolid building is now open on weekends as a general store, with tours on Sunday afternoons. Across the street awaits your first W&OD Railroad station, one of six that remain. This one is used by the Northern Virginia Model Railroaders Association as a train museum. Also at this point, the parallel equestrian trail begins.

Onward, the trail takes on a decidedly rural feel as you pass flower-filled backyards and pockets of tangled wilderness. Then, just before mile marker 13, you cross over Piney Branch on a beautiful stone arch dating back to before the Civil War. The terrain becomes rolling, a lovely niche of open fields, burbling brooks, and lowlands. Listen for frogs and watch for foxes and deer. Wild Turk's-cap lilies bloom crazily along the trail here in late July.

Just before mile marker 15, you come to a bad crossing at Hunter Mill Road. Cross the Dulles toll road just beyond mile marker 16, and enter the town of Reston, a rather interesting place in that it is a model planned community, designed in the 1960s by Robert E. Simon Jr. The basic idea is a self-sufficient urban community in a rural setting. The W&OD connects in several places with the award-winning town's system of trails. You'll find another old train station just before Reston Parkway (mile 18); it now serves as the Park Authority ranger station and has some picnic tables. Just north of the parkway is the Reston Town Center, with a bike shop and several restaurants.

Lovely countryside beckons just out of Leesburg on the Washington & Old Dominion Railroad trail.

Beyond mile marker 19, cross a second stone arch bridge and soon enter the town of Herndon, with another bad crossing at Elden Street. In the heart of town proudly stands another old train depot. Development and numerous residential street crossings mar the trail over the next few miles, as you make your way to Sterling, a late nineteenth-century commercial village overshadowed by the nearby suburban bedroom community of Sterling Park. The ruins of President Buchanan's summer White House, used in 1859 and '60, lie beside the trail here; converted into the Sterling Motel after the Civil War, it long since has fallen into decay.

Farther on you cross busy Sully Road (VA–28) at mile 24, and plunge into the lovely rolling green landscape of Loudoun County. You're in for a bit of a climb for 4 miles, sorry to say, but street crossings are few. Ashburn (mile 27.6), a popular commercial village and resort along the railroad line in 1860, was originally called Farmwell. The name was changed in 1896 after a large ash tree caught fire and burned for a week.

Proceeding along the trail, you come to a bridge spanning Goose

Creek just beyond mile marker 30. Although it has been destroyed and rebuilt several times in the past 130 years (its latest incarnation was built in 1981), its stone piers date from the original antebellum construction. Beyond mile marker 32, Tuscarora Creek plays hide-and-seek with the trail; this is a popular place to drop a line for small-mouth bass, bluegill, and perch.

And then you come to Leesburg. At busy Catoctin Circle (mile 33.8), you'll find a bike shop and several restaurants about a quar ter-mile north of the trail. The trail doesn't bring you into the pic turesque old town, but it's worth detouring on King Street to see it (see sidebar earlier in this trail narrative).

Farther on, you cross over the Leesburg Bypass (mile 35.7) and enter the heart of Virginia's fabled emerald countryside, with splendid hilly views of red barns, grazing cows, and crisp, straight lines of corn. The trail begins a gradual climb through Clarks Gap, the highest point on the trail; you've reached its apex as you cross over the VA–7 bypass (mile 38.5). Zip through wee Paeonian Springs (mile 39), a shady hamlet with charming houses dating back to the days when Washingtonians escaped here from the summer heat.

The farmland beauty of Loudoun County embraces the last 6 or so miles to Purcellville, with the misty Blue Ridge etching the horizon. At the intersection of the VA–7 bypass and VA–287 (mile 43), you make an obvious half-mile detour off the old rail bed, then zoom downhill into Purcellville, first settled in 1763. Pass the water tower (there are several restaurants and groceries about a half-mile south of the trail from here), cross a couple of picturesque village streets, and just beyond mile 45 you come to the end of the trail in downtown Purcellville. Greeting you on the left is the old, seemingly forgotten train station, its paint peeling and window panes broken, but a vivid memory of the past nonetheless.

MORE RAIL-TRAILS

Bluemont Junction Trail

This shady path connects pretty Bluemont Park with the bustling Ballston area. It's used mainly by locals for commuting or for a daily run or stroll.

Activities:

Location: From Bluemont Park on Wilson Boulevard to Ballston, in Arlington County

Length: 1 mile one-way

Surface: Asphalt

Wheelchair access: Yes

Difficulty: Easy

Food: Ballston Mall has a food court.

Rest rooms: Ballston Mall

Seasons: Open year-round.

Access and parking: Access at Bluemont Park on Wilson Boulevard.

Rentals: No

Contact: Arlington County Department of Public Works, 2100 Clarendon Boulevard, Suite 717, Arlington, VA 22201; (703) 228–3699.

Chester Linear Park Trail

This short but pretty trail is primarily used by local residents. Plans are in the works to connect it with other park facilities.

Activities:

Notes: This trail is suitable for mountain bikes and hybrid bikes.

Location: South of Richmond in central Chesterfield County

Length: 0.75 mile one-way

Surface: Gravel dust

Wheelchair access: Yes

Difficulty: Easy

Food: You'll find groceries and restaurants in the city of Chester.

Rest rooms: No

Seasons: Open year-round.

Access and parking: The southern terminus is at VA–10, west of the town of Chester. The northern terminus is at McAllister Drive, also west of town, which you can access by going west on VA–10 to Ecoft Avenue and turning right. At DeLavin Street, go right, then left on McAllister Drive. The trail head is on the left, just before Womack Road.

Rentals: No

Contact: Chesterfield County Parks & Recreation Department, P.O. Box 40, Chesterfield, VA 23832; (804) 748–1623.

Park Connector Bikeway

Running along portions of the abandoned right-of-way for the Norfolk Southern Railroad, this trail essentially explores suburban neighborhoods.

Activities:

Location: City of Virginia Beach, along Independence Boulevard and Rosemont Road

Length: 5 miles one-way

Surface: Asphalt

Wheelchair access: Yes

Difficulty: Easy

Food: In the city of Virginia Beach

Rest rooms: No

Seasons: Open year-round.

Access and parking: Park along city streets. Trail is accessible at all cross streets along Independence Boulevard and Rosemont Road.

Rentals: Seashore Bike & Hobby Shop, 2268 Seashore Shoppes, Virginia Beach, VA 23451; (757) 481–5191. Ocean Rentals Beach Service, 577 Sandbridge Road, Virginia Beach, VA 23456; (757) 721–6210.

Contact: Department of Planning, Room 115, Operations Building, 2405 Courthouse Road, Virginia Beach, VA 23456; (757) 427-4621.

Park Trail

This hike-bike trail wends through the battlefield where, on June 25, 1864, a ragtag group of some 500 old men and young boys held off 5,000 Union cavalry raiders to protect the Staunton River railroad bridge. After exploring the Confederate earthwork defenses, the trail crosses the Staunton River and follows the old Norfolk Southern right-of-way through the battlefield to Randolph.

Activities:

Notes: Mountain bikes or hybrids preferred.

Location: Staunton River Battlefield State Park in Halifax County

Length: 1.2 miles one-way

Surface: Crushed stone

Wheelchair access: Yes, although the trail can be bumpy in places.

Difficulty: Easy

Food: No

Rest rooms: The battlefield visitor center has rest rooms.

Seasons: Open year-round.

Access and parking: From South Boston, take U.S. 360 and VA–92 northeast to Route 600, located about 5 miles beyond the town of Clover. Follow Route 600 about 3 miles and turn right on Route 855; proceed to the main park visitor center, where you can park. Access also on Route 607 in Randolph.

Rentals: No

Contact: Staunton River Battlefield State Park, 1035 Fort Hill Trail, Randolph, VA 23962; (804) 454–4312.

Warrenton Branch Greenway

A section of the old Warrenton Branch of the Southern Railway has been converted into a shady greenway. Beginning behind the Depot Restaurant in downtown Warrenton, it runs to the Old Meetz Trailhead on the cul-de-sac at Old Meetz Road.

Activities:

Location: Greenway Park in downtown Warrenton

Length: 1.48 miles one-way

Surface: Asphalt

Wheelchair access: Yes

Difficulty: Easy. The trail is flat.

Food: The Depot Restaurant is located at the trailhead.

Rest rooms: No

Seasons: Open year-round.

Access and parking: The trailhead is located directly behind the old Southern Railway depot on Third Street, in downtown Warrenton. There's a small parking area there.

Rentals: No

Contact: Fauquier County Parks and Recreation Department, 62 Culpeper Street, Warrenton, VA 20186; (540) 347–6896.

Rails-to-Trails

WEST VIRGINIA

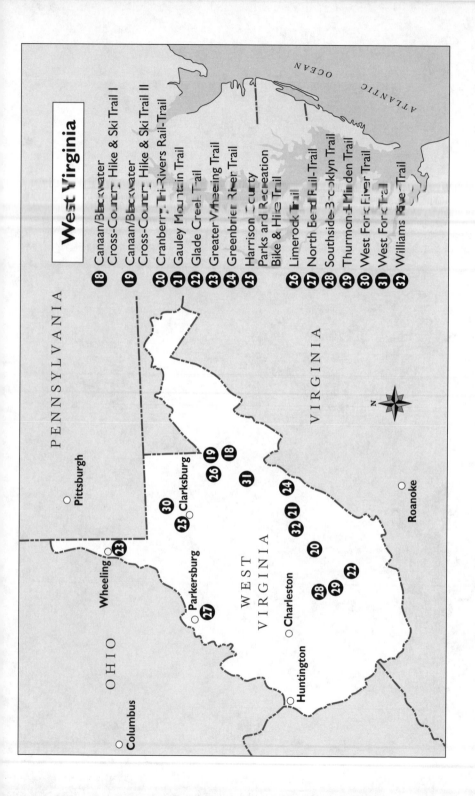

West Virginia

18 Canaan/Blackwater
    Cross-Country Hike & Ski Trail I
19 Canaan/Blackwater
    Cross-Country Hike & Ski Trail II
20 Cranberry Tri-Rivers Rail-Trail
21 Gauley Mountain Trail
22 Glade Creek Trail
23 Greater Wheeling Trail
24 Greenbrier River Trail
25 Harrison County
    Parks and Recreation
    Bike & Hike Trail
26 Limerock Trail
27 North Bend Rail-Trail
28 Southside-Brooklyn Trail
29 Thurmond-Minden Trail
30 West Fork River Trail
31 West Fork Trail
32 Williams River Trail

INTRODUCTION

The railroads came to West Virginia in the late nineteenth and early twentieth centuries to haul coal, timber, and petroleum off the mountains for East Coast cities. The vast rail network opened up gorgeous, remote corners of the state, especially throughout today's Monongahela National Forest. But there came a time when the mineral reserves were depleted; this waning, combined with the growing importance of the automobile and airplane, drummed the death requiem for many of the state's railroad corridors.

Over the past fifteen years, the popularity of rail-trails has metamorphosed these old rail lines into wonderful multiuse recreational trails. West Virginia now has more than 350 miles of rail-trails, with more abandoned rails being converted all the time. The state's premier rail-trail is the Greenbrier River Trail, snaking 77 miles through the wild Greenbrier River Valley. Other popular trails include the 70.1-mile North Bend Rail Trail, with twelve tunnels and thirty-two bridges to negotiate the harsh landscape; and the 25.5-mile West Fork Trail, which showcases a forested enclave along the West Fork Greenbrier River. But West Virginia is special in that its legacy of narrow-gauge railroads offers some unusually remote trails high in the mountains. The Limerock Trail, for instance, snakes down the timbered wall of the Blackwater River Canyon.

The citizen-based West Virginia Rails-to-Trails Council is responsible for promoting many of the state's trails, while various local organizations oversee individual projects. There always seems to be a new trail opening up, while progress is constantly being made on such ambitious endeavors as the statewide Mon River Trail. Indeed, far-ranging goals of establishing an interconnected statewide network are quickly becoming reality. For the most up-to-date information, contact the West Virginia Rails-to-Trails Council at P.O. Box 8889, South Charleston, WV 25303 or visit its Web site at www.wvrtc. org.

West Virginia's

TOP RAIL-TRAILS

18 Canaan/Blackwater Cross-Country Hike & Ski Trail I

Climbing up Canaan Mountain to its broad, spruce-sprinkled summit, this rugged rail-trail explores a less traveled route, virtually assuring glimpses of wildlife: white-tailed deer, grouse, wild turkeys, even black bears. It's beautiful year-round, but there's something magical about winter, when snow transforms the landscape into a glistening wonderland, ideal for cross-country skiing.

Activities:

Notes: Primitive camping is available throughout National Forest lands.

Location: Canaan Valley Resort State Park and Monongahela National Forest, Tucker County

Length: 3.8 miles one-way

Surface: Natural

Wheelchair access: No

Difficulty: Difficult. As rail-trails go, this one is steeper than most, but the climb up Canaan Mountain is gradual, with only a couple of steep segments. Bikers will find the trail technical with its rocks, roots, and logs.

Food: At Canaan Valley Resort State Park lodge

Rest rooms: At Canaan Valley Resort State Park lodge

Seasons: Open year-round. From late December to mid-March, snow turns this trail into an idyllic cross-country ski path.

Access and parking: Park at the lodge and follow the park road toward the golf clubhouse to the Balsam Swamp Overlook. Just up from here, you'll see the sign for the Middle Ridge Trail spur.

Rentals: Blackwater Bikes, William Avenue, Davis, WV 26260; (304) 259–5286.

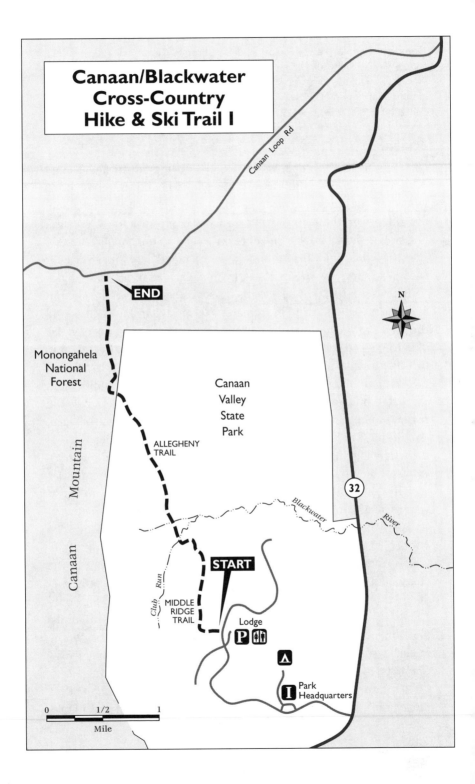

Canaan/Blackwater
Cross-Country
Hike & Ski Trail 1

Canaan Loop Rd

END

N

Monongahela
National
Forest

Canaan
Valley
State
Park

ALLEGHENY
TRAIL

Blackwater

River

32

START

Club Run

MIDDLE
RIDGE
TRAIL

Lodge
P

Park
Headquarters

0   1/2   1
Mile

Contact: Canaan Valley Resort and Conference Center, HC 70, Box 330, Davis, WV 26260; (304) 866–4121. Cheat Ranger District, USDA Forest Service, P.O. Box 368, Parsons, WV 26282; (304) 478–8251. West Virginia Division of Tourism and Parks & Recreation, State Capitol Complex, Charleston, WV 25305; (800) CALL WVA.

* *

Climbing from Canaan Valley to Canaan Mountain's plateau summit, this forested rail-trail brings you to beautiful upland bogs, where russet grasses wave in gentle breezes, tangles of rhododendron bloom bright in spring, red spruce and hemlock tower upward, and slow-moving, crystal-clear creeks reflect an enormous blue sky. In these wilds, wildlife is abundant: white-tailed deer and grouse for sure, wild turkeys, woodpeckers, even a black bear or two.

The second-growth deciduous trees you see now are lovely, but before the loggers came in the late 1800s, Canaan Mountain—and the area's other mountains as well—was covered with spectacular old-growth red spruce. In 1885 the first stock of trees was taken to the Davis mills, about 10 miles away. Davis boomed in the thirty-eight years following, hosting 3,000 timber-searching souls; more than 200 miles of timber railroads tentacled from town across the region's increasingly naked slopes. One logging officer once bragged, "We didn't leave a tree standing." Perhaps the only saving grace of the whole logging epoch are the rail beds, since converted into marvelous trails that explore some of the region's more remote areas.

This particular rail-trail follows a section of the Canaan/Blackwater Cross-Country Hike & Ski Trail, a 7.8-mile corridor between Canaan Valley Resort State Park and Blackwater Falls State Park. The Hike & Ski Trail, in turn, is a segment of the 330-mile Allegheny Trail, which runs the entire length of the state. About 80 percent of the Hike & Ski Trail follows narrow-gauge logging trails. Because the middle portion of the trail does not, the West Virginia Rails-to-Trails Council has designated the two ends of the corridor as separate rail-trails: the 4-mile section described here, and the 1.5-mile portion beginning in Blackwater Falls State Park (see Trail 19, "Canaan/Blackwater Cross-Country Hike & Ski Trail II").

Beginning in Canaan Valley Resort State Park, follow the Middle Ridge Trail spur through a beautiful forest of hemlock, cherry, maple, and black and yellow birch. Cross a stream on a boardwalk and, at the intersection with the Middle Ridge Trail, go right. This rolling pathway brings you through more woods, where the silence is broken only by white-tailed deer snapping through the understory and tall, spindly trees creaking eerily in the breeze. The trees soon give way to a pretty balsam swamp divided by mirror-smooth Club Run; here, signs at another trail intersection indicate that the Middle Ridge Trail goes left. You want to go straight ahead on the unmarked trail, arching around the swamp. A footbridge carries you across Club Run; proceed along past thick groves of rhododendron and mountain laurel and over another mountain stream. Here you come to another trail intersection, with signage indicating that you are on one trail with two names: the Allegheny Trail and the Canaan/Blackwater Cross-Country Trail. Proceed straight ahead, at last on the official rail-trail.

The forest closes in, and the trail traverses peaceful, stream-crossed woods, with rhododendron and mountain laurel flourishing everywhere. After a while you'll spot a sign denoting that you have a ⅔-mile climb as you begin your ascent up Canaan Mountain—hey, at least you were warned! Farther, another sign flags an even steeper section, and beyond this you leave the state park, entering

Club Run winds through pretty Balsam Swamp, along the Middle Ridge Trail.

Monongahela National Forest. Be sure to look off to the right, back over your shoulder, for fabulous views of Canaan Valley through the trees. This unique mountain valley is more than 3,200 feet high, cradled by peaks of the Alleghenies towering 4,200 feet high and offering a climate reminiscent of Canada.

Finally the trail levels out, the scenery opens up, and you feel like you're on top of the world. Bog grasses, red spruce, and rhododendron color the landscape bronze, gold, and green, and water runs everywhere, rushing down the mountain on the way to the Blackwater River headwaters 400 feet below. Indeed, the trail itself has a tendency to become wet, with a section where stepping-stones transport you across muck and mud.

The official rail-trail ends at the Canaan Loop Road, but, you can continue all the way to Blackwater Falls State Park.

In the heart of Canaan Valley, the Middle Ridge Trail is wide and flat; but farther ahead you begin the hike up Canaan Mountain.

Curtained by green rhododendrons and mountain laurel, this short trail travels most of its length beside a chattering, stone-speckled stream.

Activities:

Notes: Primitive camping is available throughout National Forest lands.

Location: Blackwater Falls State Park and Monongahela National Forest

Length: 1.5 miles one-way

Surface: Natural

Wheelchair access: No

Difficulty: Moderate. The first half mile is nearly flat, then begins a gradual climb up Canaan Mountain. Water in the trail is frequent here; hiking boots are recommended. Bikers should be prepared for some technical riding over roots and ruts.

Food: At Blackwater Lodge

Rest rooms: At Blackwater Lodge

Seasons: Open year-round. From late December to mid-March, snow turns this trail into an idyllic cross-country ski path.

Access and parking: Find the trailhead at the riding stables in Blackwater Falls State Park, off the park road. Upon entering Blackwater Falls State Park from Davis, you'll come to an intersection; go left, across the Blackwater River. The stables will be on your left in a mile or so.

Rentals: Rentals are available nearby:
- Blackwater Bikes, William Avenue, Davis, WV 26260; (304) 259–5286.
- Blackwater Falls State Park (304–259–5216) also rents bikes.

Contact: Blackwater Falls State Park, P.O. Box 490, Davis WV 26260; (304) 259–5216. West Virginia Division of Tourism and Parks & Recreation, State Capitol Complex, Charleston, WV 25305; (800) CALL WVA.

• •

Running through pretty rhododendron woods, Engine Run stream is named for a narrow-gauge engine that, according to local lore, once tumbled into it. Now the stream is the hallmark of this beautiful rail-trail, an easy mountain path ambling up Canaan Mountain in Blackwater Falls State Park and Monongahela National Forest. It's great for hikers and bikers both, although bikers should have a bit of technical expertise to negotiate the roots and rocks that speckle the trail.

Blackwater Falls shares the same history as Canaan Valley Resort State Park (see Trail 18, "Canaan/Blackwater Cross-Country Hike & Ski Trail I"), with loggers completely denuding its mountain slopes of timber in the late 1800s and early 1900s. Logging trains once ran along the trail you're traipsing today, carrying precious loads of old-growth trees destined for Davis's mills. After the land became part of the Monongahela National Forest, second-growth trees grew up, creating the lovely (and protected) forest you see today.

You're following a section of the Canaan/Blackwater Cross-Country Hike & Ski Trail, a 7.8-mile corridor between Blackwater Falls

State Park and Canaan Valley Resort State Park. To make things a little confusing, it runs concurrently with the Davis Trail and the Allegheny Trail (a 330-mile statewide trail), and you'll see signposts for all three. About 80 percent of the Hike & Ski Trail follows narrow-gauge logging trails. The middle portion of the trail is not on original railroad grades, and so the West Virginia Rails-to-Trails Council designated the two ends of the corridor as separate rail-trails: the 1.5-mile portion here and the 4-mile section beginning in Canaan Valley Resort State Park (see Trail 18).

Thickets of rhododendron shade the Davis Trail, a frilly delight in late spring.

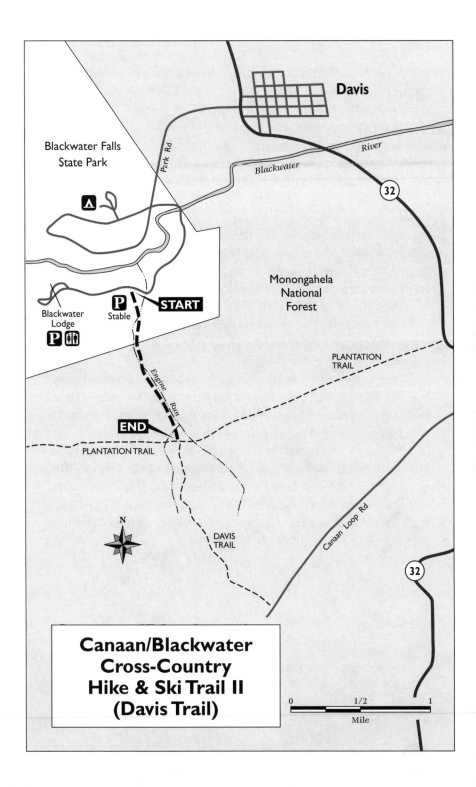

Davis

Blackwater Falls
State Park

Perk Rd

Blackwater River

32

Monongahela
National
Forest

Blackwater
Lodge

P
Stable

START

PLANTATION
TRAIL

Engine Run

END

PLANTATION TRAIL

Canaan Loop Rd

N

DAVIS
TRAIL

32

Canaan/Blackwater
Cross-Country
Hike & Ski Trail II
(Davis Trail)

0   1/2   1
Mile

There are separate trailheads for bikers and hikers; daytime parking for both is available at the riding stables. Hikers will walk behind the riding stables and head left at the DAVIS TRAIL sign, walk over Engine Run stream on a wooden bridge, then meet up with the bike trail. Bikers, meanwhile, will find their trailhead back out on the park road; turn right from the stables parking area and find the trailhead marked by two boulders there. At the point where the two trails meet, follow the signs toward the Plantation Trail and the Canaan Loop Road. Right away you're enveloped by beautiful mountain laurel and rhododendrons—easy to spot with their dark green, waxy leaves—and serenaded by the prattling stream. You come to another trail intersection, with the Steamwinder Grade Trail going to the right, over Engine Run. Proceed straight on the Davis Trail/Allegheny Trail. You leave the state park, enter the Monongahela National Forest, and the mountain laurel and hemlock close in, creating an especially pretty scene. Cross over Engine Run on a rustic bridge, then enjoy a long green wall of rhododendrons, with little pine cones and needles mixing underfoot.

About a mile or so from the trailhead, the stream has moved away, and you begin a fairly obvious ascent up Canaan Mountain. Cross over a streamlet, and brace yourself for an even steeper climb. Finally, the woods open up, and you see a six-person cabin on the right (available on a first-come, first-served basis). Just beyond awaits the intersection with the Plantation Trail, the end of the rail-trail. You can continue on to the loop road (1.25 miles) or Canaan Valley Resort State Park (6.3 miles). The challenging yet ridable Plantation Trail, by the way, is a favorite among West Virginia bikers and part of the Canaan Mountain biking races.

20   Cranberry/Tri-Rivers Rail-Trail

From the timber town of Richwood, this recently opened trail (1997) runs along three different rivers, the Cherry, the Gauley (one of the country's most famous white-water rivers), and the Cranberry. The prettiest section is beyond the Gauley–Cranberry confluence, where sweeping views take in remote corners of the Monongahela National Forest.

Activities:

Notes: A handful of primitive campsites is available; check with the Chamber of Commerce.

Location: From Richwood to just beyond Sarah's tunnel, south of Allingdale, in the Monongahela National Forest

Length: 16.5 miles one-way (no mile markers on the trail)

Surface: Crushed stone

Difficulty: Easy to moderate. The drop down to the Gauley is a breeze, but the 300-foot rise back to town should not be overlooked. Until the surface is a bit more compacted, come prepared for a bumpy ride at times (padded shorts and gel seats).

Wheelchair access: Yes. The section just outside of Richwood, paralleling the Cherry, is the smoothest.

Food: Limited. Convenience stores can be found in Richwood and Fenwick along the trail's first 6.5 miles.

Rest rooms: No

Seasons: Open year-round. Early spring's runoff brings the three rivers to life with rushing water, wildflowers, and mountains painted bright green. In winter the occasional snowfall creates a perfect blanket for cross-country skiing.

Access and parking: There are several access points along the trail:

- *Richwood:* The trailhead is just south of WV–39/55 on Oakford Avenue. Parking is available for about a dozen cars at the old, unmarked train depot, with additional parking at the nearby shopping center.
- *Fenwick:* From Richwood go northwest on WV–39/55. Access is found at the crossing of the Cherry, where WV–55 and WV–39 split. Parking is next to the post office. Proceed under the bridge to reach the confluence or upstream to Richwood.

- *Holcomb:* This is the recommended access point, to take in the best scenery. Find it by heading northwest from Richwood on WV–55/20. Parking is on the left, just before crossing the Cherry. Cross the highway and follow the trail downstream.

Rentals: Four Seasons Outfitters, WV–39/55, Richwood, WV 26261; (304) 846–4605.

Contact: Richwood Chamber of Commerce, Main Street, Richwood, WV 26261; (304) 846–6790. Gauley Ranger Station, P.O. Box 110, Richwood, WV 20201, (304) 040–2095.

• •

One of West Virginia's newest rail-trails, the Cranberry/Tri-Rivers Rail-Trail offers an opportunity to view the rugged backcountry of the Monongahela National Forest while enjoying the cool, roiling waters of three different rivers: the Cherry, the Gauley, and the Cranberry. Once you move beyond the timber towns of Richwood, Fenwick, and Holcomb, the scenery becomes remote—pure West Virginia mountain country.

A spur of the Baltimore & Ohio Railroad once ran along this route, serving the area's huge lumber market. Indeed, Richwood was established in 1901 by the Cherry River Boom and Lumber Company. Plans for the trail began in 1989 when CSX Transportation announced it was abandoning the old spur. Originally opposed to the loss of the railway, town leaders soon recognized the possibilities of the right-of-way. The railway, local timber giant Georgia-Pacific, the West Virginia Rails-to-Trails Council, a crew of volunteers, and a federal grant all pitched in to make the conversion from tracks to trail a reality.

The result of the hard work begins at the B&O Depot in downtown Richwood, off Oakford Avenue between WV–39/55 and the Cherry River. The first 6.5 miles trace the river from Richwood's center and on through the riverside towns of Fenwick and Holcomb—a medley of schools, ball fields, churches, and backyard gardens of corn and tomatoes. Because of this relatively urban setting, many choose to begin the trail at Holcomb.

Gravel clutters the first couple of miles beyond Holcomb, making for a bumpy ride. You soon leave behind the last of the buildings and houses, coming to a small wood bridge over dainty Holcomb Run (mile 7), one of the trail's many prime fishing spots. The Cherry

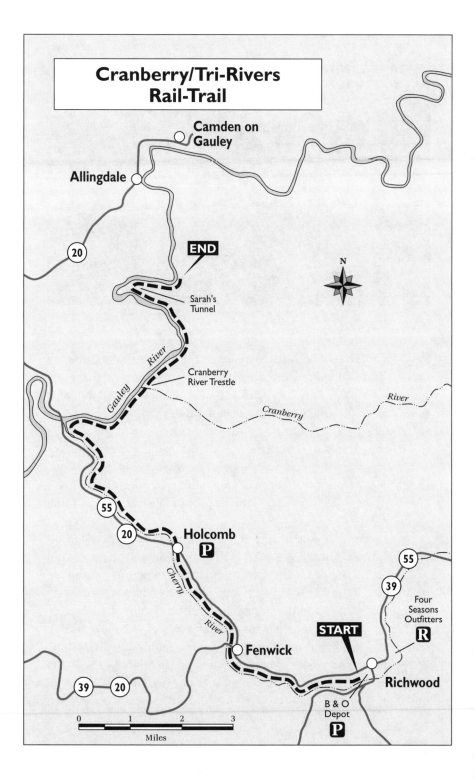

Cranberry/Tri-Rivers Rail-Trail

Camden on Gauley

Allingdale

20

END

Sarah's Tunnel

Gauley River

Cranberry River Trestle

Cranberry River

N

55

20

Holcomb
P

Cherry River

55

39

Four Seasons Outfitters
R

START

Richwood

Fenwick

39   20

B & O Depot
P

0   1   2   3
Miles

A hiker crosses the trestle above the Cranberry River.

steadily entertains with its rustle of water and, in springtime, its azalea- and rhododendron-lined banks. Unfortunately, the proximity of WV–20/55 on the opposite bank can fill the ear. Watch for remnants of the trail's previous occupant: perhaps an old railroad tie or spike.

At about mile 8, a wood platform with makeshift waterspout gives trail users access to a mountain spring, the perfect place to refill water bottles. Across the Cherry is a working reminder of the area's past: a lumber mill, impressive with its piles of sawdust and unevenly scattered logs.

In another half mile or so you reach the confluence of the Cherry and the more imposing Gauley. The surrounding flat piece of land was once the site of Curtin, a booming lumber town that extended on all sides of the rivers. Still remaining are a crumbling cement railroad signal station and the stanchions of the old railroad bridge.

This is where the route begins to climb gently. The tone and landscape change as you turn upstream on the Gauley, finally leaving behind the major roads. Cranberry Ridge and Horse Ridge rise in the foreground, and the water's echoing roar seems to mimic that of an oncoming locomotive.

The next miles yield a smoother surface. Kayakers often play in the holes and waves of the Gauley, while rafters enjoy riding its rolling rapids. Across the river, the occasional angler stands outside his cabin with rod and reel in hand, hoping for smallmouth bass, walleye, or muskellunge.

About 12 miles from the start in Richwood, you reach the perfect picnic spot: the 282-foot Cranberry River Trestle. Crossing the trail's third river, its wood planks have long replaced the legendary 1900 trestle. A young woman named Sarah was allegedly murdered here; her ghost is said to haunt Sarah's tunnel farther up the Gauley. The bridge is not the only attraction, as many anglers head to the Cranberry's confluence for its rainbow- and brown-trout-filled waters. If even you don't fish, the nearby shelter and benches make for a nice retreat. The private houses near the trail represent the remains of Woodbine/Cranberry Station, a logging community that stood here a century ago.

Behind the cabins, Rock Shelter Trail is a country road that offers a challenging 6-mile route back to Holcomb or Richwood. This is definitely not a shortcut home—the steep gravel road climbs more than 1,000 feet in less than 3 miles. Ask the Richwood Chamber for specific directions.

Although many turn back at the trestle, there is a reward of isolation for continuing upstream on the Gauley, around Perry Ridge. Until the conversion of the trail, few had access to this section of the national forest, where

The Cranberry River flows over rocky terrain near its confluence with the Gauley River.

yellow poplar, beech, birch, and maple create a rich-hued patchwork in fall. In addition to the mountains, the next 2 miles bring crossings of three intermittent streams whose waters are occasionally dammed by enterprising beavers.

The Gauley slowly bends west until you reach the trail's highlight: Sarah's tunnel. About 2.5 miles beyond the Cranberry trestle, the curving 640-foot hole makes a shortcut through the hillside to rejoin the watercourse after it's taken its own horseshoe bend. It's here that Sarah's ghost is said to haunt the darkness. Sometime around 1910, a woman called "Sarah" (not her real name) was found floating in the waters below the Cranberry trestle's tracks. No one was ever brought to justice, but lore continues that she was murdered by the family of the man with whom she was having an adulterous affair. Not quite as surreal, look through the tunnel's dimness for the several stone-and-brick notches built into the walls. These recessions served as hiding places for workers trying to escape an oncoming train (imagine the deafening sound and the rushing wind).

From here the trail continues another 2 miles before fading out a mile short of Allingdale (there is no trail, and no bridge to help you reach town). Return to Richwood the way you came. Before leaving the area, though, be sure to sample some of the other activities this recreation-rich region has to offer. Richwood is considered the "southern gateway" of the Monongahela National Forest, a hotbed for rafting, kayaking, and hiking as well as mountain biking.

The start of the Cranberry/Tri-Rivers Rail-Trail, along the Cherry River, begins as a bumpy ride.

21   Gauley Mountain Trail

One of Tea Creek's fabulous, well-maintained trails, this wide, rocky, spruce-lined rail-trail explores the remote beauty of Gauley Mountain—an especially popular mountain-biking destination.

Activities:

Location: Tea Creek Recreation Area of Monongahela National Forest, Pocahontas County

Length: 5 miles one-way

Surface: Dirt

Wheelchair access: No

Difficulty: Moderate. Despite its high elevation (4,000 feet), the trail is mostly level.

Food: Pack in your own. The nearest groceries and restaurants are in Marlinton. Elk River Touring Center, 8.8 miles north of the U.S. 219 junction with WV–150 in the community of Slatyfork, has a restaurant (plus lodging).

Rest rooms: No

Seasons: Open year-round. Cross-country skiing in winter is wonderful, although access roads are not plowed.

Access and parking: The trail is accessible at each end point:
- *WV–150:* From the junction of WV–39 and U.S. 219 in Marlinton, go north 6.9 miles on U.S. 219 to WV–150. A left on WV–150 brings you in about 5 miles to the trail's southern terminus, on the right.
- *Forest Road 24:* To reach the northern terminus, where this narrative begins, continue farther north on U.S. 219 about 7.3 miles to Mine Road/County Road 219/1 (if you reach the community of Slatyfork you've gone about 1.5 miles too far). Go left and proceed for 3.5 miles on the gravel road (which becomes Forest Road 24) to the trailhead on the left.

Rentals: Elk River Touring Center, U.S. 219, Slatyfork, WV 26291; (304) 572-3771; located 8.8 miles north of U.S. 219 junction with WV–150, in community of Slatyfork; rents skis and bikes and offers cross-country skiing and fly-fishing trips.

Contact: Assistant Ranger, Marlinton Ranger District, Tea Creek Recreation Area, P.O. Box 210, Marlinton, WV 24954-0210; (304) 799–4334.

• • • • • • • • • • • • • • • • • • •

Fabulously remote, the Gauley Mountain Trail visits the wild face of its namesake peak, in the heart of the Tea Creek Recreation Area. Even though you're high up in the mountains, the trail maintains a fairly constant elevation, making it popular with hikers and mountain bikers alike (as well as cross-country skiers). To add a bit of a thrill, you're in black bear country here; sightings of this elusive species are common.

The trails that crisscross Gauley Mountain owe their existence to the standard-gauge logging railroads that sprouted up in the early 1900s. Loggers flocked here to strip the mountainsides bare of trees and roll them away to eastern markets. Now that second-growth trees cloak the landscape, it's nearly possible to forgive those loggers, given their wonderful legacy of trails. The Gauley Mountain Trail is only one of the slew of trails that can be interconnected to create a longer wilderness experience. For starters, the Williams

Red spruce edges the wild Gauley Mountain Trail, a splendid mountain path in the Tea Creek Recreation Area.

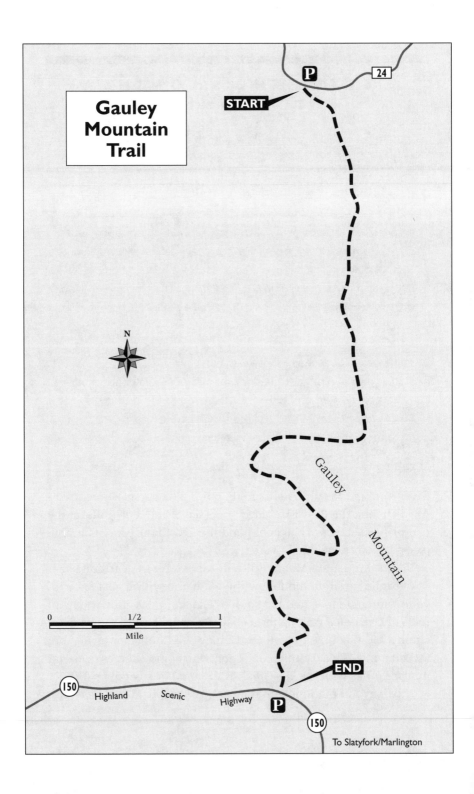

GUESS WHO'S COMING TO DINNER

If you're not careful it could be *Ursus americanus*, the black bear, West Virginia's official animal. Giant, lumbering, and wild. It's truly a thrill to sight one of these forest-dwelling beasts, although many count themselves lucky if they never get the chance. Bears are typically shy and secretive, and will rarely let you know they're around. In spring and early summer, however, black bears become more active, as mother bears encourage young bears to find homes of their own; in addition, older males roam the wilderness in search of a mate. Another thing to keep in mind is that bears have a hard time controlling themselves when it comes to food, and they possess noses that can smell dinner a long way off. If you don't take the proper precautions while camping, you may end up with uninvited guests.

Some tips:

- Do not approach bears for any reason.
- Steer clear of bears with cubs or cubs that seem to be alone. Mother bears can be overly protective.
- When camping, store food in sealed containers and keep it in the car; or, if you're in the backcountry, rope it up between two trees.

River Trail (see Trail 32) is a pretty stroll along a splashing, trout-filled stream; the Bear Pen Ridge Trail (see "More Rail-Trails" at the end of this section of the book) and the Tea Creek Mountain Trail (see also "More Rail-Trails") are here.

From the Gauley Mountain trailhead, climb the earthen barrier onto the rail-trail and follow the wide, rocky trail, shaded with yellow birch, maple, and red spruce. The ground is often wet, with roots and puddles making for a challenging bike ride. You begin to climb a bit, meeting up with the Gauley-Tea Connector just before the first mile. This 0.6-mile-long spur, with some old cross ties still in place, links with the Tea Creek Trail (another splendid path).

Just beyond the junction, the trail passes a field speckled with wood shamrock, foamflower, bluebeard lily, and painted trillium. Pass the Bear Pen Ridge Trail at mile 1.5, a 3.5-mile spur through a red spruce forest that connects with the Tea Creek Trail.

Farther ahead, the Gauley Mountain Trail continues an easy uphill, with a couple of climbs thrown in for good measure. A mile or so beyond the Bear Pen Ridge Trail, you reach the summit at 4,400 feet, along with the junction with the 2.5-mile Red Run Trail, a rocky path featuring red spruce and the head of Red Run, and ending at the Right Fork of Tea Creek Trail. The trail makes a gradual descent, with enough of a slope to make for a fast, fun bike ride. About 3.7 miles from the beginning, you enter a lovely meadow; stop and enjoy the sun's warmth and the wildflowers that flourish here in spring and summer. Then enter the woods again, descending a small hill to a wooden bridge. At mile 4.8, you pass the junction with the Right Fork Connector Trail, a 0.6-mile spur that connects with the Right Fork of Tea Creek Trail. Cross two sets of boardwalks over a marshy streambed, and proceed about 0.3 mile to the parking area at WV–150, the southern terminus.

Boardwalks crisscross swampy ground on the Gauley Mountain Trail.

Tucked away in one of the quietest and most pristine corners of the New River Gorge, this remote trail follows a crystal-clear, trout-filled stream past silvery waterfalls, rhododendron thickets, and dark hemlock forests.

Activities:

Notes: Primitive camping at Glade Creek trailhead

Location: New River Gorge National River, Raleigh County

Length: 5.6 miles one-way

Surface: Natural

Wheelchair access: No

Difficulty: Difficult. Expect several sets of stone steps before the bridge crossing at the halfway point.

Food: Pack your own. Towns outside the park have groceries and restaurants, including Hinton, Beaver, Beckley, Mount Hope, Oak Hill, and Fayetteville.

Rest rooms: Pit toilets available at Glade Creek Camping Area.

Seasons: Open year-round. Spring is divine with its new green woods and wildflowers; summer brings heat, haze, humidity, and thunderstorms; autumn, the driest season, has warm sunny days, crisp nights, and gorgeous October colors; and winter days range from mild to frigid, including blizzards and freezing rain that will make trail access difficult but offer the possibility of good cross-country skiing. The best views are in winter when the leaves are off.

Access and parking: From U.S. 19 north of Beckley, take WV–41 north toward Prince. Turn right on the Glade Creek Road just before the Prince bridge over the New River. Follow the gravel road 7 miles to the Glade Creek trailhead. There's plenty of parking, along with picnic tables and a camping area.

Rentals: Rentals are available nearby:

- Ridge Rider Mountain Bikes, Crossroads Mall, Mt. Hope, WV 25880; (304) 256–2453 or (800) 890–2453; and 103 Keller Avenue, Fayetteville, WV 25840; (800) 890–2453.
- ACE Adventure Center, P.O. Box 1168, Oak Hill, WV 25901; (304) 469–2651 or (888) ACE–RAFT.

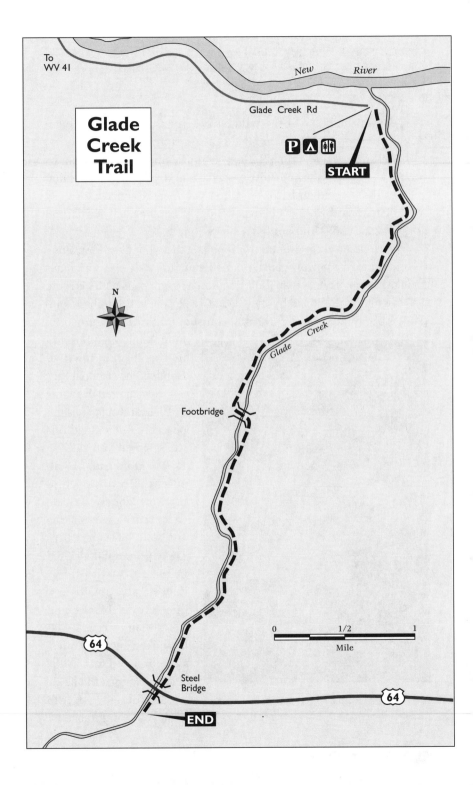

To
WV 41

New River

Glade Creek Rd

Glade Creek Trail

P ▲ 🚻

START

N

Glade Creek

Footbridge

64

0   1/2   1
Mile

64

Steel Bridge

END

Contact: Superintendent, National Park Service, New River Gorge National River, P.O. Box 246, Glen Jean, WV 25846; (304) 465–0508.

• • • • • • • • • • • • • • • • • • • •

Deep in the heart of the wild New River Gorge hides an even wilder corner, known as Glade Creek. Here, a hemlock-shaded pathway runs beside a rushing, ice-clear stream, ragged mountains scrape a primal sky, waterfalls cascade into deep green pools, and visitors are few and far between. This is an incredible trail for those wishing to escape from, well, everything except the purity of nature. For that's all you'll find along its entire length.

The isolation comes much from the fact that you're walking along the old route of a narrow-gauge railroad, built to tackle steeper grades and narrower corridors than their traditional freight cousins. This route was originally developed by the Glade Creek Coal and Lumber Company Railway in the early 1900s. It transported timber from nearby

mountaintops to the mill in the former town of Hamlet. The National Park Service acquired the gorge in 1978, and since has impeccably maintained this well-marked trail.

The trailhead is located at the confluence of the New River and Glade Creek, surrounded by the ghost town of Hamlet. This sawmill outpost flourished in the 1920s with thirty houses, a post office, a three-story clubhouse, and a physician's office. All collapsed during the Depression, and the forest has since reclaimed the land.

Maples, hemlocks, and rhododendrons shade Glade Creek in the remote New River Gorge.

Starting off on the trail, you're embraced by

A hiker enjoys a quiet spot along rugged Glade Creek.

hemlocks and maples, rhododendron thickets, and pockets of wood betony and maidenhair fern. The only sound comes from the wind riffling through the tall treetops, and the cascading creek chattering beside you—your constant companion the entire way. The trail climbs and winds through the forest, the domain of white-tailed deer and black bear, wild turkey and bobcat. In about a mile awaits an overlook of the creek, followed by a grand waterfall. Scramble up some steps, then enjoy a level stretch of trail, where several deep green pools beckon anglers (trout are stocked several times a year).

By mile 2 you'll be scrambling around more rocks, and in the next mile be treated to more waterfalls splashing into shadowy, foliage-twisted chasms. At about the 3-mile point, a footbridge arches across Glade Creek, providing a good prospect both up- and downriver. Onward, in about 1.5 miles, you'll meet up with the 1.6-mile Kates Falls Trail, which leads to the 4.0-mile Kates Plateau Trail and 4.1-mile Polls Plateau Trail, making for a longer hike (obtain a trail map from the Glen Jean ranger station).

And that's about it. There's one more powerful waterfall; then the huge steel bridge that carries I-64 over the New River Gorge jars you from this luscious serenity. That's okay, turn around and escape back into the woods, enjoying it all anew.

23 Greater Wheeling Trail

Traveling along the mighty Ohio River through the heart of Wheeling, this urban rail-trail reflects both the industrial and natural faces of the historic waterway. Part of a still-growing rail-trail system in the area, plans include extending the trail into Ohio County.

Activities:

Location: From Pike Island Locks and Dam to 48th Street, city of Wheeling in Ohio County

Length: 9 miles one-way

Surface: Asphalt

Wheelchair access: Yes. Handicapped-accessible parking areas at WV–2 in the north end of Warwood, Twelfth Street in downtown Wheeling, and Thirty-fifth Street in South Wheeling.

Difficulty: Easy. The level trail is smooth and fast.

Food: Never far from the trail.

Rest rooms: No public rest rooms along the trail.

Seasons: Open year-round.

Access and parking: Access and parking are available at both end points and all along the trail:

- *Pike Island Locks and Dam:* To reach the northern terminus at Pike Island Locks and Dam, take WV–2 (River Road) about 6.5 miles north from downtown Wheeling.
- *Forty-eighth and Water Streets:* The southern terminus is south of downtown Wheeling at 48th and Water Streets.
- *Throughout Wheeling:* Trail access is almost continuous throughout the city, with parking available on city streets and in parking garages; parking areas are located at Pike Island Dam, WV–2 at the north end of Warwood, North Ninth Street in Warwood, and Thirty-fifth Street in South Wheeling.

Rentals: No

Contact: Wheeling Convention and Tourism Bureau, 1401 Main Street, Wheeling, WV 26003; (304) 233–7709 or (800) 828–3097. Greater Wheeling Trails Coalition, 116 Valley Boulevard, Wheeling, WV 26003.

• •

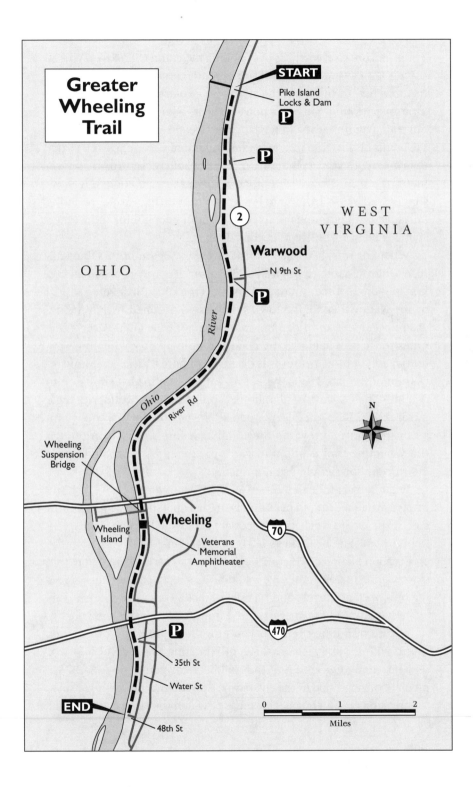

Greater Wheeling Trail

START
Pike Island Locks & Dam
P

P

2

WEST VIRGINIA

OHIO

Warwood
N 9th St
P

Ohio River

Ohio River Rd

Wheeling Suspension Bridge

Wheeling Island

Wheeling
Veterans Memorial Amphitheater

70

470

P
35th St
Water St

END
48th St

N

0   1   2
Miles

S tacked on wooded bluffs overlooking the grand Ohio River, Wheeling is first and foremost a nineteenth-century industrial town.
Its focus has always been the river—for exploration, for navigation,
for transportation, for water power. The river is also the focus of this
rail-trail. Beginning at a huge dam, the Greater Wheeling Trail traces
the banks of the Ohio past factories and homes, churches and parks,
offering river vistas at every turn. A marvelously flat thread of pave-
ment, the trail is hugely popular with locals, who come out in all
shapes and sizes, from grizzled, cigarette-puffing valilev pedaling
one-speeds, to pram-pushing mothers, to fit young men and women
sporting New York City marathon T-shirts.

Wheeling was the western terminus of the Baltimore & Ohio Railroad when it came to town in 1852 to service area coal mines and
iron foundries. Already a port of entry on the Ohio River being served
by the National Road, the town's industry quickened. When the de-
cision was made to bridge the railroad across the Ohio River a few
miles south of Wheeling, any chance to fully realize Wheeling's potential as a railroad center was dashed. Hit hard by the economic re-
cession of the late 1850s, Wheeling—and its railroads—slipped into
decline. The network of abandoned spurs has left a wonderful legacy for modern-day trail users. Indeed, the city has an extremely ambitious program to revamp these rail beds into rail-trails. Although
the Wheeling trail is still a work in progress, it's estimated that a
quarter-million people use it annually.

Begin north of the city limits on Warwood Avenue (WV–2), at the
impressive Pike Island Locks and Dam. It's open twenty-four hours a
day, seven days a week, so chances are good you'll catch a barge lock-
ing through. The best views of this navigational ballet are from the
observation platform. The trail begins near the parking area; note that
since work is ongoing, mileage markers are simply painted lines across
the trail, with no corresponding mile number. For easy reference, this
narrative refers to mileages counted from the locks and dam.

Taking off along the trail, you enter a realm of nature scenes
mixed with industry, the essence of Wheeling, indeed. A bounty of
benches along the length of the trail beckons you to pause and ap-
preciate the wild side of the riverscape—its singing birds, shy turkeys,
scampering ground hogs—as well as to watch the river traffic motor

by, from colossal barges to tiny dinghies top-heavy with anglers.

Around mile 2 you enter a green space, then pass by flower-filled backyards in the community of Warwood. The residential feel turns more industrial in the next mile or two as you pass Warwood Tool Company and Intertech International, both on the right, and then the sky-blue Wheeling Watertower. Beyond the Centre Foundry & Machine Company, with its yards full of industrial appurtenances, you come right alongside Warwood Avenue, which immediately becomes busy River Road. Not the prettiest setting, but carry on.

Beyond mile 4 pass Citgo 76, with an intriguing old building surely dating back a century. By mile 5 you will spy development on Wheeling Island, in the middle of the river. Listen for the tolling of church bells announcing the quarter hour, the bass notes echoing across the river.

Farther, a great old redbrick church marks your arrival into North Wheeling, known as Victorian Old Town. You won't see them from the trail, but this neighborhood is known for its glorious Victorian houses. Chief among them is the Eckhart House, at 810 Main Street. (Contact the Convention & Tourism Bureau for tour information.) As you get into Wheeling proper, a cement wall and greenery separate

Across the Ohio River, Wheeling Island's Victorian houses recall the city's nineteenth-century industrial boom.

you from the city bustle, letting you focus on the beautiful river. In the warm summer twilight, the water shimmers gold as the sun slips beyond the dark island hulk beyond. On Wheeling Island you can pick out some of the beautiful Victorian mansions lining the river-bank.

Around mile 6 you get your first glimpse of the green arches that carry I–70 across the waterway, with the black-cabled Wheeling Suspension Bridge looming beyond. Pass by Wheeling Yacht Club, go beneath the I–70 bridge, and then beneath the venerable old bridge itself. The first bridge built across the Ohio River, and once the longest bridge in the word (1,010 feet), the Wheeling Suspension Bridge opened in 1849 to the fanfare of citizens attired in their Sunday best. It was a vital link in the National Road, the first federally financed interstate highway that became the major route for east-west travel across America. With its imposing hand-cut stone towers, graceful cables, and distinctive suspenders, the bridge is the nation's most important extant engineering structure built before the Civil War.

Ahead, you come to the Veterans Memorial on the left, with a gray stone sphere topping a column, and the Veterans Memorial Amphitheater on the right, which offers a chance to sit by the river and admire the bridgescapes. The amphitheater is the jewel of the historic waterfront, all of which is being redeveloped as part of the Wheeling National Heritage Area. The ambitious $50 million project is scheduled for completion in the year 2000.

Passing by the Civic Center, you are in the heart of Wheeling's revitalizing downtown. Forming the backbone of Heritage Square, the visitor center and the Artisan Center (housed in a restored industrial building and offering authentic Wheeling and West Virginia crafts) stand just on the other side of the Civic Center.

At the other end of downtown, cross the mouth of Wheeling Creek on a renovated trestle. According to legend, in the early 1700s it was here that the scalped head of a white trader was affixed to a pole, warning other traders to stay away. The name of Wheeling derives from the Delaware language meaning "place of the head."

By mile 7 you have cleared downtown, traversing an area of old factories in Center and South Wheeling: an old grocery supply depot, the old Mail Pouch Tobacco building—all in lovely red brick.

This area is slated to be redeveloped; many of the old buildings are to be retrofitted for new office space. Pass by an industrial yard, move alongside timeworn railroad tracks, and pass beneath another great bridge. Around mile 8, wrap around the softball diamond of Wheeling Middle School, then pass by a mix of backyards and factories along Water Street. At Forty-eighth Street, the trail ends . . . for now.

In addition to the north-south section described above, there is an east-west portion of the trail. It begins at the riverfront amphitheater and weaves east along downtown streets, passing by some of Wheeling's best examples of period architecture. Beyond the East Wheeling neighborhood and a century-old railroad tunnel, the connecting portion is not yet complete; you'll have to follow Mount DeChantal Road to Washington Avenue. Here the trail picks up again, passing Wheeling Hospital and some beautiful views of Wheeling Creek, and ending at the edge of Wheeling's Elm Grove neighborhood.

24 Greenbrier River Trail

The queen of West Virginia's rail-trails, and one of the longest and most scenic in the country, the Greenbrier River Trail parallels the rapid-filled Greenbrier River in a landscape punctuated by tall peaks. Winding through the Greenbrier River Valley, it visits a blend of dark forests and steep cliffs, small towns and plush pastures, with souvenirs of its railroading days including thirty-five trestles and long-forgotten whistlestops.

Activities:

Notes: Twelve rustic campsites are available along the trail. Additional camping at nearby Cass Scenic Railroad State Park, Watoga State Park, Greenbrier State Forest, Seneca State Forest, and Blue Bend Recreation Area. Paddlesports here includes canoeing. A popular canoeing put-in is Sitlington Creek, just upstream of bridge on opposite side of trail. The run from Sitlington to Marlinton is good for canoe novices. A popular dayhike is Marlinton to Buckeye and back (8 miles round-trip).

Location: Between Cass and Caldwell, in Pocahontas and Greenbrier Counties

Length: 77 miles one-way

Surface: Original ballast, made of mostly hard-packed gravel and rock, with one short section of limestone chips between Renick and Horrock (the limestone came from Renick Rock Quarry near mile 26)

Wheelchair access: The 2-mile section south of Marlinton depot is blacktopped for wheelchairs.

Difficulty: Moderate. North to south is slightly downhill.

Food: This is a true mountain trail, with services few and far between. Make sure to bring along food and water. You'll find food in the following places:
- Cass State Park (northern terminus), snack bar, restaurant in old country store.
- Marlinton (mile 56.1), stores and restaurants.
- Buckeye (mile 52.1), grocery along U.S. 219.
- Seebert (mile 45.7), convenience store; meals at Watoga State Park on east side of river from Seebert bridge.
- Renick (mile 24.7), groceries.

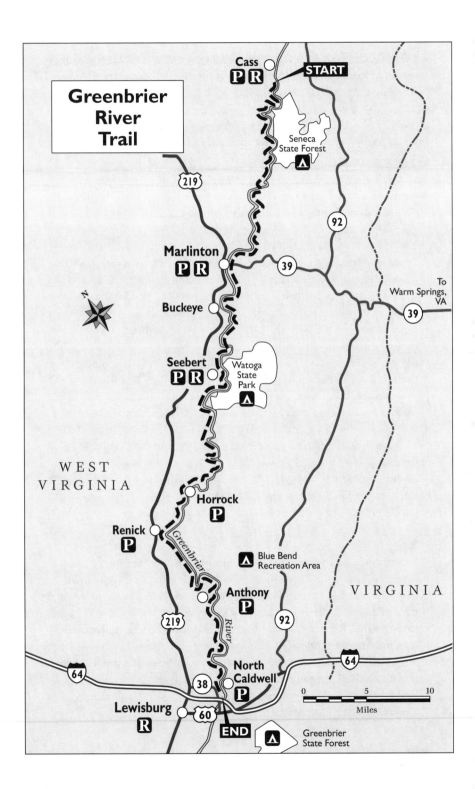

Greenbrier
River
Trail

START

Cass
P R

Seneca
State Forest

219

92

Marlinton
P R

39

Buckeye

To
Warm Springs,
VA

39

Seebert
P R

Watoga
State
Park

WEST
VIRGINIA

Horrock
P

Blue Bend
Recreation Area

Renick
P

VIRGINIA

Greenbrier

Anthony
P

92

219

River

North
Caldwell
P

64

64

38

0   5   10

Miles

Lewisburg
R

60

END

Greenbrier
State Forest

- North Caldwell (southern terminus), from the Caldwell trailhead, the closest food (food marts and fast food) is at the North Caldwell interstate intersection, east on U.S. 60.

Rest rooms: A few along the trail, including at Cass State Park (northern terminus), Marlinton visitor information center (mile 56.1), Stillwell Park (mile 55.7), and the roadside park in Buckeye (mile 52.1).

Seasons: Open year-round. Be aware of hunting seasons; hunting is never allowed on Sundays. Spectacular color along length of the trail in early October.

Access and limited parking: There are many access points along the trail:
- *Cass* (northern terminus): From Elkins, follow U.S. 250 south to WV–28/92. Go south 10 miles to WV–66 and turn west, to the park. The rail-trail begins across from the country store.
- *Deer Creek* (mile 79.5, the first access point below Cass suitable for bike access): From Cass, go about half a mile on WV–66 to Deer Creek Road, turn left, and proceed half a mile to the end of the road at the old Deer Creek stop, where the hard-packed trail begins.
- *Stony Bottom* (mile 74.3): From Cass, go west on WV–66 and south on County Road 1 (Back Mountain Road).
- *Clover Lick* (mile 71.1): From U.S. 219, 3.6 miles north of Marlinton, take County Road 1 (Back Mountain Road). Or from WV–28, 2.6 miles south of Dunmore, take County Road 1/4 (Laurel Creek Road). Also accessible from Snowshoe via County Road 9 and from Cass via County Road 1.
- *Marlinton* (mile 56.1): Access at Main Street (County Road 39) and Fourth Avenue. Park at the restored railroad depot (Pocahontas County Tourism Office).
- *Buckeye* (mile 52.1): From U.S. 219 south of Marlinton, take Old Buckeye Road, turn right 100 feet, and go a quarter mile to the trail. Overnight parking is not recommended, as this is a local hangout.
- *Watoga bridge* (mile 47.9): From Marlinton go south on U.S. 219 to County Road 219-8; take this to County Road 27, and go right to access road on left.
- *Seebert* (mile 45.7): Take U.S. 219 south of Marlinton to County Road 27 (Seebert Road), 1 mile north of Hillsboro. Or from County Road 39 at Huntersville, take County Road 21 (Watoga Park Road); proceed through park to bridge.
- *Denmar* (mile 39.3): Go south of Marlinton on U.S. 219 to Hillsboro; here turn left on County Road 31 (Denmar Road). Or, from U.S. 219 south of Marlinton, take County Road 20 (Locust Creek Road); turn left at intersection and go 3.1 miles.
- *Beard* (mile 38.5): Go south of Marlinton on U.S. 219 to Hillsboro; go left on County Road 31 to Beard.

- *Horrock* (mile 29.6): From U.S. 219 south of Marlinton, take County Road 7 (Brownstown Road) in Renick; 5.4 miles from Renick turn right at the 150-degree turn; limited parking.
- *Renick* (mile 24.7): From U.S. 219 south of Marlinton, go left on County Road 11 (Auto Road) for 0.4 mile; parking beside trail.
- *Spring Creek* (mile 21.6): From U.S. 219 south of Marlinton, take County Road 13 (Spring Creek Station Road) 1.5 miles north of Frankford. Also accessible from Renick.
- *Anthony* (mile 14.1): From U.S. 219 at Frankford, go left on County Road 21 (Anthony Creek Road) and County Road 21/2; parking beside trail. Also accessible via Blue Bend Road from County Road 92 at Avlon.
- *North Caldwell* (southern terminus): From Lewisburg, take U.S. 60 east to the west end of the Greenbrier River bridge at Caldwell. Here follow County Road 38 (Stone House Road) north for 1.4 miles; parking area at southern trailhead.

Rentals and shuttle services: Rentals as well as shuttle services are available nearby:
- High Country Connections, HC 61, Box 156, Cass, WV 24927 (800–245-3798), offers bike tours, rentals, and log cabin lodging; located 2 miles east of Cass on WV–66.
- Appalachian Sport (mile 56.1), 3 Seneca Trail N., Marlinton, WV 24954 (304–799-4050), rents bikes and canoes.
- Jack Horner's Corner convenience store (mile 45.5) on Seebert Lane, in Seebert (304–653-4515), rents bikes.
- Woods, Water and Wheels Bikeshop, 200 West Washington Street, Lewisburg, WV 24901 (304–645-5200), rents bikes and canoes, and offers shuttle services.
- Free Spirit Adventures and Bike Shop, 104 Foster Street, Lewisburg, WV 24901 (304–645-2093 or 800–877-4749), rents bikes and offers shuttle services.
- Greenbrier River Campground, P.O. Box 265, Ronceverte, WV 24970 (800–775-2203), offers a shuttle service to the trail, plus biking, canoeing, fishing, and tubing tours on the Greenbrier River.

Contact: Superintendent, Greenbrier River Trail, Star Route, Box 125, Caldwell, WV 24925; (304) 536–1944.

• • • • • • • • • • • • • • • • • • • •

Coursing through the wild heart of West Virginia beside the Greenbrier River, this spectacular rail-trail explores the domain of black bears and beavers, white-tailed deer and painted turtles. In this splendid backcountry, the rugged Alleghenies rise 4,000 feet, so steep that the lands between them are called "hollers," and eight rivers are born among them. Along the way, a handful of mountain towns built on the area's lumber craze serve as respites, offering up B&Bs and a glimpse into the region's past.

The Greenbrier Division of the Chesapeake & Ohio Railroad was built through here a century ago, as part of the state's vast 3,000-mile network of logging railroads. Small towns sprang up overnight, each boasting a cookie cutter depot, wood frame houses, and plenty of jobs. For twenty years the rail line transported timber from the surrounding hills. Later, as the timber supply was depleted, the line became an important passenger link between the East and Midwest. The last passenger train ran in 1958, with freight being carried for twenty more years. The corridor was abandoned in 1978, and donated to the state of West Virginia. While the trail experience is essentially natural, not historic, many of the original mileposts serve as reminders of bygone days. Whistlestops, too—thinner markers with W carved and painted on one side—stand as memories of a time when train engineers would be reminded to blow their whistles (two long, one short, one final long blast) to warn people and animals of the approaching train.

Most people agree that it's best to begin a jaunt at the northern terminus, at the Cass Scenic Railroad State Park, to take advantage of the gentle 752-foot drop along the trail. (You can arrange a shuttle to return.) This is the direction this narrative takes. One thing to remember is that the mileage markers originate at the southern end, so you'll be counting down rather than up.

You'll love Cass, a company town of beautifully renovated houses connected by catwalks. To get into the railroading mood, take a ride aboard the steam locomotive up Cheat Mountain, West Virginia's second highest peak. Along the town's old main street you'll find a country store that sells almost anything you would need related to railroading, timber company houses restored as quaint accommodations, as well as rest rooms, a post office, and public phones and drinking water.

The rail-trail begins just across from the Cass Country Store; you'll see right away that the ties and rails are still in place, making riding

CHARMING LITTLE
LEWISBURG

Seemingly out of place amid the rugged Alleghenies, Lewisburg is a charming little town that belongs more in the Vermont countryside than far-off West Virginia coal country. But there it is, an absolutely adorable eighteenth- and nineteenth-century village with some of the most intriguing boutiques, art galleries, country inns, and restaurants around. Its proximity to the southern terminus of the Greenbrier River Trail makes for a perfect stopover before or after a trail ride.

Lewisburg can trace its roots to 1751, when a young surveyor, Andrew Lewis, established a camp near a spring behind the present-day courthouse. This spring has been known as Lewis Spring ever since. The town was chartered in 1792, and still features a venerable collection of antebellum structures. On the square, the Old Stone Church (1796) is the oldest church west of the Alleghenies remaining in continuous use; the headstones of some of the area's early settlers can be found in the surrounding cemetery. Nearby, the 1820 John A. North House depicts the comfortable lifestyle of an early settler.

But what makes this town so alluring is its dichotomous personality—between past and present, country and cosmopolitan. Lording over all these interesting but none-too-special historic buildings, for instance, is the stately, columned, extremely refined Carnegie Hall, donated by steel magnate Andrew Carnegie in 1902. Its 500-seat performance hall and exhibition spaces have recently undergone a $3 million restoration. It shines. And there's little fiddlin' going on here—only the cosmopolitan strains of the likes of Isaac Stern and Ricky Skaggs.

Take a stroll downtown for another sampling of the town's split personality. Here, traditional antique shops mingle with New Age stores; old-fashioned barbershops shoulder nouvelle-cuisine restaurants. It's fun just to poke your head into shop after shop, to see what there is to see. And that's the fun of it—you'll always be surprised. Maggie's is a New Yorkesque café

(continued)

featuring soothing music, artwork on the walls, and the pungent aroma of fresh-ground coffee. Across the street, Clingman's Market serves up huge heapings of delicious country-style glop in an old butcher shop. On a side street you'll find the old aqua-and-white Victorian that houses Julians Restaurant & Coffee Bar—dedicated to using only the freshest ingredients, and fearless to experiment with unexpected flavors. Marinated bay shrimp with fennel, and grilled Georgia chicken with peach chutney and sweet potatoes were on a recent menu.

And then there is the art. Some of the downtown shops purvey the expected homespun crafts, but there is an admirable collection of galleries that hang only discriminating works, explaining why Lewisburg was recently nominated one of the nation's top one hundred art towns.

For more information, contact the Lewisburg Convention and Visitors Bureau, 105 Church Street, Lewisburg, WV 24901; (304) 645–1000 or (800) 833–2068.

difficult. If you're on a bike, it's better to detour about half a mile on WV–66 to Deer Creek Road, turn left, and proceed half a mile to the end of the road at the old Deer Creek stop. There is parking available for cars and horse trailers here.

Taking off, you're engulfed by oaks and maples and pines, and right away you are sure to spot some of the region's abundant wildlife: groundhogs, deer, snakes, squirrels, and chipmunks especially. For the next few miles there are several trestles crossing small streams. South of Sitlington (mile 76.8), the trees of Seneca State Forest fringe the far riverbank. At mile 74.4 you pass through the crossroads of Stony Bottom, where Moore's Motel provides rooms, and a service station up County Road 1 has a cold drink machine, your last chance for a refreshing soda for nearly 20 miles.

The trail's first improved campsite lies at mile 69.6, surrounded by a dense growth of ferns. At mile 65.2, you come to the stone-faced Sharps Tunnel, at 511 feet the longest (and straightest) tunnel along the trail. Emerging from the cool, dank darkness, you cross over the trail's first major bridge, its four spans hovering 30 feet above the Greenbrier. The 229-foot structure, built in 1900 by the Pencoyd Iron Works in Pennsylvania, offers spectacular views of the winding Greenbrier River Valley, and is a popular fishing spot for locals. At its south end, step down the retaining wall to a niche by the river ideal for picnicking, swimming, and tossing a line in hopes of small- and largemouth bass, sunfish, rock bass, catfish, walleye, pike, muskie, or trout.

South, the trail climbs high on the river's east bank, exploring thick green forests and intermittent farms. Another improved campsite awaits at mile 63.7. You know you're approaching Marlinton, about 7.5 miles farther, as you glide by the trail's only remaining railroad water tower (mile 56.5).

The only major town along the trail, Marlinton, at mile 56.1, was founded in 1749, making it the oldest settlement west of the Alleghenies. The Pocahontas County Museum just south of town on U.S. 219 fills in some of the historical facts. The town's pride and joy is the bright red caboose and red-and-yellow depot, built in 1901. A portion of the depot now serves as a tourist information office. The town itself is rather quaint, with restaurants, groceries, and lodging.

Just south of Marlinton, at mile 55.7, cross over Knapp's Creek bridge. Built in 1889, it connects Marlinton to Stillwell Park across the river, which offers camping and public toilets. You quickly leave the houses behind, entering a beautiful landscape splashed with spring and summer wildflowers.

Just before the town of Buckeye, watch for the former section house, a company-owned

Bikers pedal along the Greenbrier River Trail in Greenbrier County.

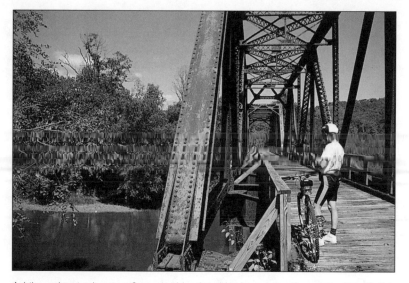

A biker takes in the view from an old railroad bridge on the Greenbrier River Trail in Pocahontas County.

house where the section foreman resided. Each section foreman was responsible for the maintenance of a portion of railroad, usually about 10 miles in length. Buckeye, at mile 52.1, offers McNeill's Country Mart & Ashland Station, Graham's Motel, and other facilities along U.S. 219, about a half mile from the trail. To reach them, turn right off the trail at Buckeye, cross a narrow bridge, and continue about half a mile on County Road 219 until you have a choice of turning right or left. Go left for 0.1 mile and you will be on U.S. 219; you can see the facilities from here. The roadside park has public toilets and picnic tables.

You pass another campsite at mile 49.3, at the mouth of Beaver Creek, featuring a backwater beside the trail that's full of rock bass. Farther along, before mile 48, watch for the ruins of the town of Watoga. They're not the easiest thing to spot: From milepost 48, go upriver about 0.1 mile to the first gated drive on the right. Just past this is the old bank safe, its rusty door still swinging on its hinges. Several paths upstream lead through the old town site (now private property), tangled with weeds and bushes and fringed with old fruit trees.

Farther down the trail, you cross over to the Greenbrier's west bank on the Watoga bridge (mile 47.9), built in 1886 and the southernmost major bridge along the trail. On the bridge's other side a short path wends down to the river's translucent waters. Look for the old beaver lodge across the river.

In about 2 miles lies the town of Seebert, at mile 45.7. Jack Horner's Corner convenience store, right by the trail, has all kinds of camping and biking supplies. Farther south, the isolated trail wedges between the hillside and the Greenbrier, bordered by the trees of Watoga State Park across the river (between mile 45.2 and 39.2). One of West Virginia's oldest state parks, it features log-and-stone cabins, hiking trails, campgrounds, and a restaurant and camp store. (The campground, restaurant, and store are some 3 miles from the Seebert bridge on the east side of the river; no access back to the trail without backtracking.)

Watoga's forest merges into the wild enclave of Calvin Price State Forest at mile 39.2. To get to or return from this beautiful parkland, ford the river at Burnsides and follow an unimproved road downriver to a second ford back to the trail at Denmar. The water can be high and fast in spring and fall, so use caution.

There's a primitive campsite at Mill Run Station (mile 40.8), about a mile below Burnsides. At mile 39.3 you pass the old Denmar State Hospital for the Chronically Ill, now a state correctional facility. The trail from here to Beard, for something different, is graded with limestone chips. In Beard (mile 38.5), you'll find the charming Current Bed & Breakfast (304–653–4722). Occupying a 1905 farmhouse, its cozy rooms and hot tub make an ideal overnight for those biking the entire trail.

You enter an especially remote section of trail south of Beard, void of stations or other signs of the lumber industry that once prospered here. Steep hills crowd the trail's right side, while mountain views extend beyond the Greenbrier on the left. A number of primitive campsites dot the trailside over the next couple of miles.

Droop Mountain Tunnel awaits at mile 30.9, its dark maw swallowing you in blackness. Actually just 402 feet long, the tunnel's bend obliterates the other portal, making it seem more ominous than it really is.

There's trail access and parking at the hamlet of Horrock (mile

29.6), a campsite at mile 28.5, and the little hamlet of Renick at mile 24.7. Here, about a half mile to your right on Auto Road (County Road 11), is the intersection with U.S. 219, where you'll find Field's Gas and Grocery and R&V Grocery, featuring clean rest rooms, groceries, and water.

The countryside between Renick and Anthony (miles 24.7 to 14) is spellbinding. Thick forest and steep mountains embrace the trail, an especially lush setting for spring and summer wildflowers. A cow pasture borders the trail between Renick and Spring Creek, offering the chance to spot some bovines up close. Farther, watch for places where you can go down to the river and boulder-hop across its pellucid green waters.

Between Anthony and North Caldwell (miles 14 to 3), the scenery

Bikers dismount for the trek across a swinging bridge suspended over the Greenbrier River in Greenbrier County.

takes in a medley of thick woods, hay fields, dramatic red shale cliffs rising straight from the trail bed, and the ever-present river. On warm summer days the river is crowded with tubers and anglers—what a great life! A campsite at mile 13, at the base of a cliff, allows you to linger overnight.

You know the end of the trail is near when you see Camp Allegheny's parking lot (mile 3.5), and its green-and-white camp buildings across the river. Soon Old Stone House Road (private) begins paralleling the trail. Look up the hill to the right to see the house that gives the road its name.

The trail ends at milepost 3, at a small park in North Caldwell, with parking, (rotting) picnic tables, and drinking water. Here you're about 1.3 miles north of U.S. 60, on County Road 38. If you take U.S. 60 east to the north Caldwell interstate intersection, you'll find gas stations, food marts, and a McDonald's, the closest facilities to the southern terminus.

Nearby are the charming historic town of Lewisburg, full of B&Bs and exquisite restaurants; White Sulphur Springs, home of the venerable Greenbrier Hotel; and the star-studded "ceiling" and pine-scented "rooms" of Greenbrier State Forest (2 miles east on U.S. 60). Take your pick.

Not the most alluring destination, this rail-trail follows the murky green West Fork River past farmland, woods, and tiny communities.

Activities:

Notes: Biking this trail requires a mountain bike or hybrid.

Location: Between Clarksburg and Spelter, Harrison County

Length: 6 miles one-way

Surface: Cinder

Wheelchair access: Yes, wheelchairs with big wheels will have no problem.

Difficulty: Moderate

Food: None along the trail, but there are restaurants and grocery stores in the city of Clarksburg.

Rest rooms: No

Seasons: Open year-round.

Access and parking: As of this writing, the only major access point is at the southern terminus in Clarksburg. To reach it from I-79, follow U.S. 50 west to the West Virginia Avenue exit. Go right on Nineteenth Street, left on Williams Street, then right on north Twenty-fifth Street. Drive past Rolland Glass Company to the marked trailhead. Street parking is available.

Rentals: No

Contact: Harrison County Parks and Recreation Commission; (304) 624-8619

• •

A relatively new trail, the Harrison County Trail traces the banks of the West Fork River north of Clarksburg, exploring wildflower-dotted fields, wooded hillsides, and several rural communities. As of this writing, the first couple of miles are nicely developed with mile-posts, benches, and a picnic pavilion; plans are in the works to augment these facilities the rest of the way. Furthermore, the northernmost mile has been closed since 1996, to clean up heavy metal in the soil adjacent to the railroad corridor. This closure is expected to continue

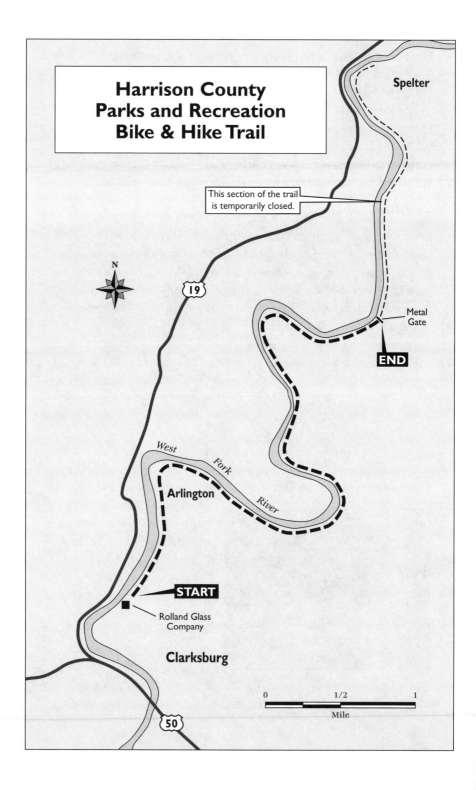

Harrison County Parks and Recreation Bike & Hike Trail

Spelter

This section of the trail is temporarily closed.

N

19

Metal Gate

END

West Fork River

Arlington

START

Rolland Glass Company

Clarksburg

0   1/2   1
Mile

50

for several years—in the meantime, you'll have to begin in Clarksburg.

The trail has its origins in the B&O Railroad, which built this line along the West Fork River (actually the West Fork Monongahela River but never called that) in the early part of the twentieth century to haul out coal and timber. As resources dwindled, the line eventually became obsolete. In 1983 the B&O donated the abandoned rail corridor to the state of West Virginia; the Harrison County Parks and Recreation Commission now leases the right of way from the West Virginia State Railroad Authority.

From the trailhead, start off above the muddy green West Fork River—your constant companion the entire way—with wooded hillsides rising on the right. In half a mile, you pass a picnic table and bench. Just beyond mile 1, cross a little road, go around a gate, and pass by several houses in the community of Arlington. Enter a wildflower-dotted corridor of green, passing an observation platform overlooking the river at mile 1.6.

Just beyond mile 1.75, cross a road. The trail continues alongside the road, but is especially bumpy—it's better to take the road instead. In a quarter of a mile or so the trail crosses the road again (if you took the road, get back on the trail here). The trail then passes through a little trailer-house enclave, with plenty of signs warning that this is private property!

You then enter a fairly isolated stretch of pretty greenery, wildflowers, and butterflies. At one point, where the river picks up some speed, the trail has been littered with tires, rusted metal gadgets, and

The woodlands are lush along the Harrison County Parks and Recreation Bike & Hike Trail.

other junk. Ick. Enjoy a nice sunny stretch, then round a hillside, where tiny paths wander across the floodplain to the river down below.

Soon you'll see Spelter's buildings and a factory ahead. The scenery opens up, you lose the river, and, at mile 6, suddenly are confronted with a metal gate—you have no choice but to turn around.

Gradually descending from the rim to the bottom of Blackwater Canyon, with spectacular views unfolding at every turn, this old railroad grade explores an extremely remote, rugged, breathtaking mountainscape.

Activities:

Location: Southwest of Thomas in Monongahela National Forest, Tucker County

Length: 4.5 miles one-way

Surface: Natural

Wheelchair access: No

Difficulty: Difficult. This area is remote. Bikers will find this a very rugged trail; all but most skilled riders will have to portage around some areas. Suspension systems are recommended.

Food: There are no services; pack in food and water. The closest groceries and restaurants are in Davis and Thomas.

Rest rooms: No

Seasons: Open year-round, although snow may make access difficult in winter. Avoid this trail after heavy rains. Suspension systems are advisable for bikers; bikers and hikers alike should wear long pants spring through summer to keep trailside nettles at bay.

Access and parking: Be forewarned: A four-wheel drive is recommended. To reach the northern trailhead from Thomas, follow County Road 27 (located near the Exxon station) through the hamlets of Coketon and Douglas. The road enters the Monongahela National Forest, becoming Forest Service Road 18, full of ruts and several stream crossings. About 5.6 miles total from Thomas, you'll see the trailhead marked on the left; it's about a quarter mile beyond the Tub Run crossing.

Rentals: Blackwater Bikes, William Avenue, Davis, WV 26260; (304) 259–5286.

Contact: Cheat Ranger District, Monongahela National Forest, P.O. Box 368, Parsons, WV 26287; (304) 478–3251.

• •

Without a four-wheel drive, the journey to this rail-trail's trail-head along the pockmarked, rock-embedded, stream-crossed forest service road may very well be the most difficult part of the entire Limerock Trail. That said, this quiet path down the steep side of Backbone Mountain to the Blackwater River is a glorious journey. Fabulous views unfold of Canaan Mountain across the valley; clear, icy streams race down the mountain slope, hurtling over and around rocks in miniature waterfalls; rhododendron blooms festoon the trail side in spring; and the thunder of the Blackwater River accentuates as you descend. Chances are slim you'll meet anyone along the way; just deer, squirrel, grouse, snakes, and—since this is black bear habitat—the rare black bear.

Hikers will love this trail; bikers too, if you're into tons of rocks and roots and boulder-choked runs. Be forewarned that tangles of thorny vines make the trail a bit painful spring through fall; long pants are recommended. One last thing: The entire trail descends into the canyon; after you turn around, you must climb back out. Rest assured that it's gradual. Certainly worth the effort, anyway.

You have to ask, in this gorgeous setting, what enticed loggers to destroy such a landscape. Money, of course. Still, there's something overpowering about this mountainscape that demands respect. Respect that logging trains somehow ignored as they chugged along the canyon wall in the early 1900s, toting load after load of fallen old-growth trees to the nearby Davis mills. But like most of the old railroads in West Virginia, their gift is the wonderful trail here today.

The return hike on the Limerock Trail is uphill, but gradual. Canaan Mountain rises in the distance.

Leaving the narrow parking area on Forest Road 18, the blue-blazed trail plunges into a

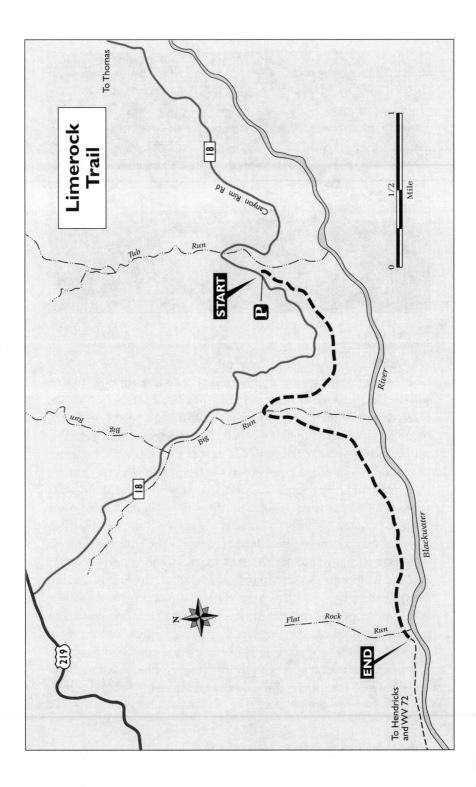

Limerock Trail

To Thomas

18

Canyon Rim Rd

Tub   Run

START

P

Big   Run

Big   Run

18

River

Blackwater

219

N

Flat   Rock

Run

END

To Hendricks
and WV 72

0   1/2   1
        Mile

Big Run is just one of the tributaries rushing down Backbone Mountain to the Blackwater River.

dark hemlock and spruce grove. In less than a tenth of a mile, it turns right along the old railroad grade and begins its run along the ridge. You can hear—and glimpse—Tub Run rushing to your left, behind a curtain of rhododendrons; limestone rocks that gave this trail its name speckle the trailside. Across the valley rises Canaan Mountain, its rounded peak etching a deep blue sky. You cross a couple of trickling tributaries, and after a while hear the distant roar of the Blackwater rising from the valley depths below. After 1.6 miles comes Big Run, its surging waters often impassable after heavy rains; otherwise, boulder-hop across. The trail continues a wee bit upstream; look for the trail marker (which also indicates that the Blackwater River is a half mile farther; the Flat Rock Trail 2 miles). Passing through a damp, dark realm of ferns and mosses, you come to another rocky tributary, its clear waters dashing around smooth boulders. A flat boulder here makes a perfect resting perch. You cross another tributary a bit farther on, ever descending gradually down the mountainside. Bit by bit the forest floor becomes more green, carpeted with ferns and dainty white and purple flowers in spring, and great white oaks tower sky-high. Cross another little tributary, and then, briefly, through the trees, you can make out the Blackwater River winding across the canyon floor—still amazingly far below!

After a while you cross another little tributary, and are treated to more glimpses of the Blackwater. A little later, the landscape seems to flatten as you enter a pretty cove and cross two more tributaries, one of which is Flat Rock Run. The trail rounds a ridge, then switchbacks down into another cove. And then, just like that, you come to the end of the trail at a former CSX railroad line, now the Blackwater Canyon Railroad Grade Trail. This is not an official rail-trail due to some complicated boundary issues, but hikers and bikers still use it. If you turn right it will take you 2.1 miles to Hendricks and WV–72; a switchbox, signal light, and the beginning of double tracks are at 1.4 miles. Ahead the Blackwater shimmers through the trees, but you can only reach it by scrambling down the wooded hillside.

West Virginia's showcase trail, the North Bend Rail Trail passes through spectacular wilderness settings and rural farmland, with several stops in small towns where artists fashion handblown glass. Wildlife proliferates, including beavers, deer, chipmunks, and, in spring and summer, hosts of songbirds.

Activities:

Location: Between Parkersburg and Wolf Summit in Harrison, Doddridge, Ritchie, and Wood Counties

Length: 70.1 miles one-way

Surface: Four types of surface, including the smooth, crushed limestone finish of the model sections, well-packed dirt and small gravel, midsize gravel, and rough and unfinished.

Wheelchair access: Yes, in places. The five model sections of trail, running from Cairo to Cornwallis, Ellenboro to Pennsboro, West Union to Smithburg, and Industrial to Bristol, are accessible. Wet conditions make passage more difficult.

Difficulty: Moderate. The trail is level with generally good surfaces, although the rough surface at the extreme ends of the trail makes the going difficult for bikers.

Food: Facilities are limited. Each of the trail's towns features a variety of restaurants, delis, and grocery stores on or near the trail. North Bend State Park also has food. Be sure to replenish your water supply when passing through towns.

Rest rooms: Facilities are available in town sites and at North Bend State Park.

Seasons: Open year-round. Most heavily traveled from May through October. Temperatures in spring and fall make for ideal conditions. Winter conditions are far from ideal; often wet, muddy, or snow-covered and icy.

Access and parking: The trail is accessible from U.S. 50 along much of its length. Major access points are:

- *Happy Valley Road, Parkersburg:* From I–77, take WV–47 east, and immediately turn right onto old WV–47 for 0.7 mile. Turn right on Happy Valley Road and go 0.3 mile to the western terminus of the trail. Park on the right-hand side of the road.

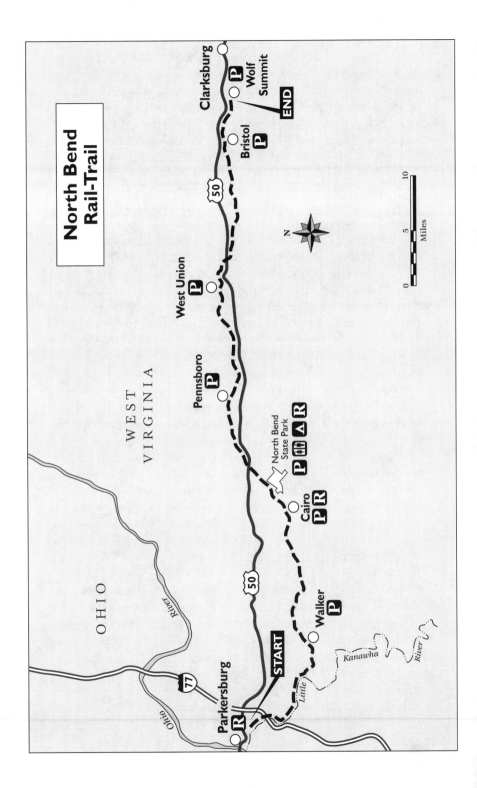

North Bend Rail-Trail

- *Walker:* From I–77 in Parkersburg, go east on WV–47, turning right immediately onto old WV–47. Go about 7 miles, turn left on Walker Road, and follow this about 7 miles until the trail crosses the road. The rail-trail is visible from Walker Road for several miles before the trailhead.
- *Cairo:* Take U.S. 50 east of Parkersburg to WV–31; then go 4 miles south into Cairo. Trail crosses WV–31 in town. Parking available on the left in front of the bike shop, on the right beyond the trail along WV–31, and on Sundays in the bank parking lot beyond the trail. Keep in mind that on warm spring and fall weekends, Cairo is often the most crowded trailhead along the trail; if there is no parking, proceed on WV–31 to the turnoff to North Bend State Park.
- *North Bend State Park:* Take U.S. 50 east of Parkersburg, exiting south on WV–31. Follow signs through Cairo to North Bend State Park. (Or take U.S. 50 west from Clarksburg, exiting south on WV–16 at Ellenboro. Follow signs through Harrisville to the state park.) At the park entrance, go past the main lodge, following signs to the campground. At the campground, turn left across bridge into the recreation area. Parking is available along the road through the recreation area. On bicycle or foot, you'll then have to follow the road through the recreation area to a half-mile-long access trail past a picnic shelter; this will bring you to the NBRT.
- *Ellenboro:* Take U.S. 50 east from Parkersburg, exiting north on WV–16. Parking lot is 0.25 mile on the right just beyond the trail overpass. If trailhead parking is full, public parking is available along town streets to the east of the trail overpass.
- *Pennsboro:* Take U.S. 50 east of Parkersburg; at WV–74 go north 1 mile to the B&O Depot.
- *Greenwood:* Take U.S. 50 east of Parkersburg to the Greenwood exit, and follow the exit road about half a mile; park at the West Virginia Department of Highways or at the Greenwood Motel. The trail is behind the motel.
- *West Union:* Take U.S. 50 east of Parkersburg to WV–18, and go north to West Union. Cross under the trail trestle, visible from U.S. 50, and turn right to the athletic field or left to town.
- *Smithburg:* Take U.S. 50 east of Parkersburg to Smithburg; turn right at the bottom of the hill onto Old U.S. 50, and proceed 0.5 mile to the B&O Depot and Spencer Park. Parking available in front of the depot or at the park.
- *Salem:* Take U.S. 50 east of Parkersburg to WV–23; go south into Salem, with parking and trail access at the B&O Depot.
- *Bristol:* Take U.S. 50 east of Parkersburg to Raccoon Run Road; the trail crosses the road immediately after exiting U.S. 50. Park alongside the trail or at the nearby bike shop.

- *Wolf Summit:* From U.S. 50 east of Parkersburg, take the Wolf Summit exit north; the exit immediately crosses the trail.

Rentals: Rentals are available nearby:

- North Bend State Park, Route 1, Box 221, Cairo, WV 26337; (304) 643–2931 or (800) CALL–WVA.
- Country Trails Bikes, Main Street, Cairo, WV 26337; (304) 628–3100.
- Bob's Bicycle Shop, 2207 Camden Avenue, Parkersburg, WV 26101; (304) 424–6317.

Contact: North Bend Rails to Trails Foundation, Inc., P.O. Box 206, Cairo, WV 26337; (800) 899–NBRT. Park Superintendent, North Bend State Park, Route 1, Box 221, Cairo, WV 26337; (304) 643–2931 or (800) CALL–WVA

• •

Winding among quiet farms, gently flowing streams, and rhodo-dendron-filled valleys, the North Bend Rail Trail (NBRT) visits one of West Virginia's quietest, most rugged corners. It's part of the 5,500-mile Delaware-to-California American Discovery Trail, which will eventually link historic and natural landmarks from coast to coast. Along the way, memories of the trail's railroading past include a collection of extremely dark tunnels—one is reputed to be haunted—and tiny towns built during the railroad's heyday.

The rail-trail has its roots in the years before the Civil War, when the Baltimore & Ohio Railroad laid tracks between Clarksburg and Parkersburg. To carry the rails through the harsh landscape of rugged ridges, boulder-strewn streams, and deep hollows, the railroad built twelve tunnels and thirty-two bridges, which remain today. The railroad serviced the regional lumber, coal, and petroleum industries, as well as transported passengers. In the late 1980s, CSX Corp. abandoned the rail line; the conversion has progressed since the early 1990s, largely due to the hard work of the North Bend Rails-to-Trails Foundation.

The trail's western terminus is at Parkersburg, but the first 10 miles to Walker are still under development and therefore extremely rough going. Only the more adventurous hikers and bikers will want to tackle the large pieces of gravel along this length.

It's better to begin your jaunt in the town of Walker, at mile 10. Indeed, as soon as you hit Walker, you'll notice that the trail surface changes to smooth crushed limestone—a delight to ride. This is one of several short sections of "model trail" that the state has developed in each county, giving an idea of what trail proponents are aspiring to do.

Leaving Walker, the trail's riverine nature is quickly evident as you cross a tributary of Walker Creek at mile 10.5, and then Walker Creek itself at mile 11.5. Soon you enter the dark maw of Tunnel #21. (The tunnels retain their original numbering from railroad days and decrease from west to east.) Also known as the Eaton Tunnel, it's the trail's second longest, at 1,040 feet. Right away you'll see why flashlights are recommended along this trail. The tunnel's curve makes it extremely black; standing, icy water comes as a shock to the unsuspecting.

A mile beyond the tunnel, the NBRT crosses Eaton Road, then, within another mile and a half, meanders across Goose Creek. Snug along the creek at mile 16.9 is the tiny town of Petroleum. After oil was discovered here in the 1890s, the town boomed. But all is quiet now, the small post office being the only souvenir of those wild days.

Half a mile east of town, Goose Creek ripples on your left; watch for the pond that traces the trail's right edge, where beavers, frogs, and birds are often active. After crossing a private gravel road nearly

A biker exits one of the North Bend Rail-Trail's twelve tunnels.

2 miles farther east, you enter a long, straight section of trail perfumed of blackberry and raspberry. Deer and rabbits often forage here.

Ferns soon become prevalent, and then a slight bend leads into Silver Run Tunnel (Tunnel #19, 1,376 feet). Train engineers used to report sightings in the tunnel's blackness of an eerie ghost-woman wearing a flowing white dress. There have been no recent appearances, but your imagination in this long, dark hole will make you believe otherwise.

Nearly 3 miles beyond the tunnel, at mile 24.1, you cross

A young mountain biker studies the rough walls of one of the North Bend Rail Trail's many tunnels.

over the North Fork Hughes River, the trail's namesake. Now begins another model trail section as you enter the town of Cairo. Crossing Main Street, watch for the bike shop facing the trail; it offers repairs, rentals, and a place to refill your water bottle. One interesting place here is the R. C. Marshall Hardware Co., an 1890s hardware store specializing in hard-to-find, turn-of-the-century tools and railroad memorabilia.

Continuing east of Cairo nearly half a mile, you enter a deep rail cut bedecked with purple columns of joe-pye weed, basil, and Deptford pink. Farther along, at mile 26.8, the trail passes through Cornwallis, another old boomtown.

Six-tenths of a mile beyond Cornwallis, you enter 1,405-acre North Bend State Park, adjacent to the North Fork Hughes River and incorporating a forested backcountry and numerous recreational facilities. A sign marks the gravel access trail that branches to the right (south) and leads 0.75 mile to the state park's campground. The park also offers bike rentals, groceries, food, and cabin rentals. Just beyond this junction, Tunnel #13 (577 feet) provides relief from the afternoon sun.

Four picnic sites dot the next 2 miles of trail, and then a long, dark pond formed by the original railroad grading borders the trail for nearly half a mile to damp, brick-lined Tunnel #12 (577 feet). Reemerging into daylight, you soon parallel Hushers Run in the shade of towering sycamores.

Two miles farther stands the Dick Bias Tunnel (Tunnel #10), which honors the work of a North Bend Rail Trail visionary. The 377-foot-long tunnel is hewn from solid rock, creating a cavelike quality. The trail continues with the air of a shaded lane for the next mile, as it bores through sycamore, white pine, and poplar. On the trail's north side at mile 30.5, Hobo Rock and Spring is a spring that pours into a hand-carved rock, a popular place to stop and get refreshed. Drink long, because ahead lies the NBRT's steepest grade, on an overpass crossing WV–16.

East of the overpass lies Ellenboro, where several glassmakers line the trail, including Mid-Atlantic of West Virginia. Here you can watch workers heat and spin their molten works into beautiful vases, marbles, and other creations. The trail wends through an urban terrain of fast-food joints, Little League fields, and manufacturing buildings. Watch for the rail cut beneath County Road 50/39, which once was Tunnel #9; in summer bluebirds often flit and frolic among the trees here.

A few cranks of the pedal bring you to another tunnel, this one brick-lined and dry. A mile beyond, a former B&O train depot signals your arrival at Pennsboro. Here, Old Stone House is the region's first permanent residence; it welcomes visitors as the local history museum, much as it did during its century-long incarnation as an inn. Several eateries have hung out their shingles to welcome trail users.

Pick up the rail grade again across the street from the train depot. Almost a mile beyond town, at mile 38.1, you reach brick-lined Tunnel #7 (779 feet), dating from 1862. Exit into shady stands of oak and maple, where quiet travelers are likely to see deer, chipmunks, and squirrels. The wooded realm soon gives way to pastoral vistas, as trees yield to hay fields and rock outcrops are replaced by rustic barns to the north.

In the vicinity of the North Fork Hughes River crossing (mile 40.1), pause and listen for summer songbirds. Half a mile beyond the river, you enter a 2-mile stretch of residential neighborhoods that comprise Toll Gate and Greenwood. East of Greenwood, the verdant West Virginia woods take over again, with shaded stands of hardwood broken by sunny patches of sumac and cattails. In spring, a riot of wildflowers includes black-eyed Susan, primrose, yellow snapdragon, and lavender. Just before you reach the tiny town of Central Station, two farms dominate the trailside: the first an old farmhouse and barn on the left, the second newer and well maintained.

Beyond Central Station at mile 46.9, pause after crossing Arnold Creek and breathe in the southerly view of meadows and stream, certainly one of the most beautiful vistas along the NBRT. Ahead looms Tunnel #6, which, at nearly half a mile long, is pitch-black. Still have that flashlight? Beyond the tunnel, the trail crosses Middle Island Creek and enters the town of West Union at mile 49.8. Here, a bike shop on the trail offers the chance to check the air in your tires before cruising the model section of trail from West Union to Smithburg.

The 2.7-mile stretch to Smithburg begins with the NBRT's longest trestle bridge. Once safely across Middle Island Creek, you wind through a forest of elm, sycamore, and maple, where deer rustle the understory. In summer, Queen Anne's lace, wild rose, and purple thistle border the trail. In Smithburg, the small, red B&O depot has been restored by the local historical society and beckons with benches. A grocery store is next to the post office, and Spencer Park offers a picnic area and five primitive campsites.

Leaving Smithburg, the NBRT plays cat and mouse for some 4 miles with U.S. 50. Entering Long Run Tunnel (Tunnel #4, 846 feet) at mile 56.7, you leave U.S. 50 behind; the tunnel's east end deposits you in a forest

Mountain bikers travel along the North Bend Rail Trail.

humming with the melodies of doves, songbirds, and cicadas.

A mile or so beyond, the landscape becomes less scenic—alternately residential and cut-over woodland—as you approach the town of Industrial. Be careful of erosion damage to the trail where logging has been excessive. Beyond the Department of Corrections facility on the trail's left side, you encounter a sign for the town of Salem. Chartered in 1794, this quaint little place overflows with Victorian architecture.

The trail runs between the stone-strewn Salem Fork and Main Street, where banks, groceries, lodging, and restaurants are available. One and a half miles east of town, the Edgar Matthey shelter is a shady picnic site with floral beds.

In Bristol, half a mile farther, bike rentals and campsites are available. The trail follows the course of a stream before entering an open, grassy area and approaching the trail's last tunnel, the 1,086-foot-long Tunnel #2. It then meanders along the remaining 3.7 miles of trail to Wolf Summit.

Traveling high above the crashing rapids of the New River, this popular, leafy trail offers fantastic views at every turn. The rails and ties that still line the old rail bed (making for a bumpy bike ride) reflect the park service's philosophy to preserve as much history as possible.

Activities:

Notes: Whitewater rafting is popular on the New River.

Location: New River Gorge National River

Length: 6 miles to Brooklyn, 7 miles to Cunard; one-way

Surface: Natural

Wheelchair access: No

Difficulty: Easy hiking, moderate biking. Although the trail is fairly level, tree roots and old railroad ties make for a bumpy bike ride.

Food: Towns outside the park have groceries and restaurants, including Hinton, Beaver, Beckley, Mount Hope, Oak Hill, and Fayetteville.

Rest rooms: Portable toilet at parking area.

Seasons: Open year-round. Spring is divine, with its new green leaves and wildflowers; summer brings heat, haze, humidity, and thunderstorms; autumn, the driest season, has warm sunny days, crisp nights, and gorgeous October colors; and winter days range from mild to frigid, including blizzards and freezing rain. There are better views in winter when the leaves are off the trees.

Access and parking: There are two major access points:

- *Thurmond Depot Visitor Center:* From U.S. 19 north of Beckley, take the Glen Jean–Thurmond exit. Take an immediate left, and go 0.5 mile to Glen Jean (site of park headquarters, open weekdays only, where you can obtain maps and other trail information). Take a right on WV–25 and follow signs toward Thurmond. Continue on this road for 6 miles to a three-way intersection. The parking area is located right before the bridge to Thurmond.
- *Cunard River Access Road:* You can also begin at the northern terminus on the Cunard River Access Road. From U.S. 19 north of Beckley, take the Main Street exit in Oak Hill. Turn right and go 0.4 mile. Take a right on

Gatewood Road and go 5.4 miles to the Cunard turnoff. Turn right and go 1.8 miles. Follow signs indicating Cunard River Access.

Rentals: Rentals are available nearby:

- Ridge Rider Mountain Bikes, Crossroads Mall, Mt. Hope, WV 25880; (304) 256–2453 or (800) 890–2453; and 103 Keller Avenue, Fayetteville, WV 25840; (800) 890–2453.
- ACE Adventure Center, P.O. Box 1168, Oak Hill, WV 25901; (304) 469–2651 or (000) ACE=RAFT.

Contact: Park Headquarters, PO Box 246, Glen Jean, WV 25846-0246; (304) 465–6524 (closed weekends)

• •

This entire rail-trail is a front-row seat above the raging New River, North America's oldest river and one of the East's premier white-water runs. Ambling through lacy green woods past weed-tangled railroad ties, stunning rocky cliffs, and patches of brilliant wildflowers, you are constantly serenaded by the great river's bass notes, punctuated by the sweet warbles of songbirds. The trail surface is smooth and the grade is mild, but there are lots of tree roots, rocks, and old rails and ties that make sections bumpy and not especially good for beginning bikers. Also, you are at times extremely close to the cliff edge—*please exercise caution.*

The rail-trail you're traveling on was originally an isolated track built by the Chesapeake & Ohio Railroad to prevent Norfolk and Western from building farther downriver. Then, in 1889, as the coal town of Thurmond boomed across the New River, the C&O built a bridge to the river's "southside," connecting the isolated track with the C&O coal line. Several mines once operated along this route, including Rock Lick, Weewin, Rush Run, Red Ash, and Brooklyn. Their foundations and coke ovens lie in ruins amid tangled vegetation, testimony to the days of King Coal. The National Park Service acquired the gorge in 1978 and since has impeccably maintained this well-marked trail.

The trailhead is somewhat hidden. From the parking lot (with a portable toilet), go up an embankment, across the road leading to Thurmond, across the railroad tracks, to the sign that says SOUTH-SIDE JUNCTION. In the early twentieth century, the river's south side was the site of the famous Dun Glen Hotel (1901–1930), fabled

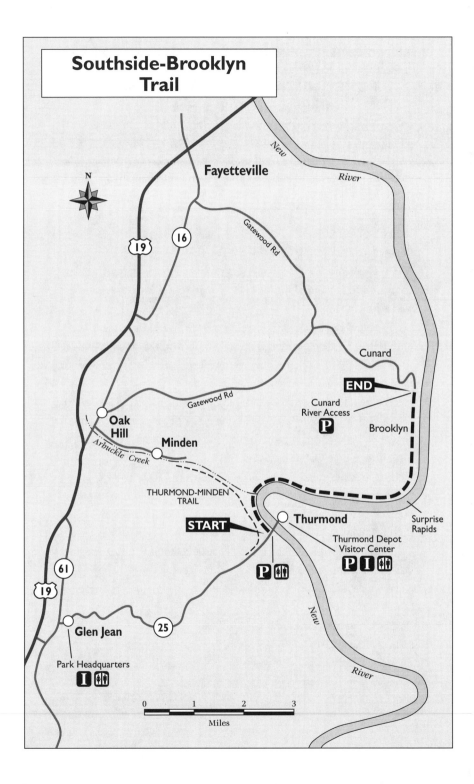

Southside-Brooklyn Trail

N

Fayetteville

New River

19

16

Gatewood Rd

Cunard

Gatewood Rd

END

Cunard River Access
P

Brooklyn

Oak Hill

Arbuckle Creek

Minden

THURMOND-MINDEN TRAIL

Thurmond

Surprise Rapids

START

Thurmond Depot Visitor Center
P I

P

61

19

New River

Glen Jean

25

Park Headquarters
I

0   1   2   3
Miles

THE NEW RIVER GORGE
IN A NUTSHELL

If the New River is the second oldest river in the world (after the Nile), why is it called the New? According to the history books, some lost explorer came upon it and dubbed it "New"—it was to him, anyway. In fact, the New can be traced to the Jurassic period, about 180 million years ago. Then, it was the main headwaters for the long-gone rivers that geologists call the Teays, which flowed westward to an inland sea. Over the eons, the landscape changed—the highlands became a plain, which in turn was uplifted and folded to create mountains. Meantime, the New continued to cut through the slowly rising ground, holding its unusual westward course.

The New has its source in North Carolina's Blue Ridge, winding north through the rugged mountains and lush farmlands of Virginia and West Virginia. Some 250 miles from its beginnings, it joins with the Gauley River to form the Kanawha, a tributary of the Ohio.

The best place to experience the New's strength and age is between Hinton and Gauley Bridge in West Virginia. Here it charges through a heavily wooded gorge, and is protected by the National Park Service as the New River Gorge National River.

Fabled for its beauty and valued in the early 1900s for its coal and timber reserves, the gorge has become one of the nation's outstanding outdoor destinations. Indeed, the three rail-trails described in this guide (Glade Creek Trail, see Trail 22; Southside-Brooklyn Trail, see Trail 28; and Thurmond-Minden Trail, see Trail 29) provide a sampling of the spectacular activities the gorge has to offer, including some of the nation's best white-water rafting and rock climbing, not to mention mountain biking, hiking, and camping.

For further information, contact park headquarters at New River Gorge National River, P.O. Box 246, Glen Jean, WV 25846; (304) 465–0508. Visitor centers are located at Canyon Rim (open daily), and at Thurmond, Grandview, and Hinton (open daily in summer, weekends only off-season).

domain of prostitution, gambling, and violence. One gambling game is said to have lasted fourteen years. From here, the dirt single-track trail takes off through mixed deciduous forest. Right away, you'll see the old ties and rails on the left, several lines of them indicating that this spot was once a switching station. Soon, the New River greets you on the right, your constant, albeit noisy, companion the rest of the way. Off to the right a great iron bridge spans the ancient river, leading to the old railroad town of Thurmond. You can make out the town's lopsided old structures teetering on the far, steep hillside, harking back to the days when Thurmond was an important shipping point for coal and when coal barons resided here.

Farther ahead awaits a wooden trestle above Arbuckle Creek, right before which a spur trail connects with the higher-level Thurmond-Minden Trail (see Trail 29), another spectacular banquette above the New River.

The trail crosses a tiny road and proceeds onward with fabulous views; be sure to check over your shoulder now and again to see what's unfolding there too. Rocky cliffs rise on the left, embellished in spring with colorful, errant wildflowers. Old rails and ties make

This biker negotiates old crosses and ties on the Southside-Brooklyn Trail.

for a rather bumpy bit of trail for bikers, then it evens out. Go over an itty trestle, and then a larger one over a creek. In summer listen for the jubilant cries of rafters as they hit Surprise Rapids a bit downstream, the first of the big white water on the lower gorge trips. Then brace yourself for another bumpy stretch, climb up and over a hill, and relax as things calm down a bit as the trail smooths, the river quiets, and once again bird melodies fill the air.

Then more rails and ties, another hill, another quiet section, and one last set of bumpy ties. At last you come to a road; this is Brooklyn, and still part of the rail-trail. From here, the road is a pretty ride, though quite rutted in places and extremely muddy after heavy rain. The best parts are the paths that snake down to the river's edge, where you can sit and watch the water flow by; anglers come to cast for smallmouth bass, walleye, striped bass, and muskellunge in the waters here. You can go about a mile farther to Cunard, where the park service has built a beautiful facility for rafters.

29 Thurmond-Minden Trail

Tunneling through thickets of rhododendron, this gently climbing trail above Dunloup Creek, the New River, and Arbuckle Creek crosses five trestles. Several overlooks provide breathtaking scenes of the old railroad town of Thurmond and of the mountain-nuzzled New River.

Activities:

Notes: Mountain bikes or hybrids are recommended for biking this trail.

Location: New River Gorge National River, Fayette County

Length: 3.4 miles one-way

Surface: Dirt and gravel

Wheelchair access: No

Difficulty: Moderate. There's a subtle uphill in the direction of Thurmond to Minden.

Food: Towns outside the park have groceries and restaurants, including Hinton, Beaver, Beckley, Mount Hope, Oak Hill, and Fayetteville.

Rest rooms: Portable toilet at trailhead

Seasons: Open year-round. Spring is divine with its new green woods and wildflowers; summer brings heat, haze, humidity, and thunderstorms; autumn, the driest season, has warm sunny days, crisp nights, and gorgeous October colors; and winter days range from mild to frigid, including blizzards and freezing rain. Views are better when the leaves are off the trees.

Access and parking: The trail can be accessed at either end point:

- *Thurmond:* To access the Thurmond trailhead, the direction this narrative takes, follow U.S. 19 north of Beckley. Take the Glen Jean–Thurmond exit, take an immediate left, and go 0.5 mile to Glen Jean (where park headquarters, open weekdays only, offers maps and other trail information). Take a right on WV–25 and follow signs toward Thurmond. The parking area and trailhead are on the left, 5.1 miles down WV–25.
- *Minden:* To access the Minden trailhead from U.S. 19 north of Beckley, take the Main Street exit (Oak Hill), turn right, and go 0.1 mile. Turn right onto Minden Road, and follow this 2.1 miles. Take a right across a small bridge to the parking area and trailhead.

Rentals: Rentals are available nearby:

- Ridge Rider Mountain Bikes, Crossroads Mall, Mt. Hope, WV 25880; (304) 256–2453 or (800) 890–2453; and 103 Keller Avenue, Fayetteville, WV 25840; (800) 890–2453.
- ACE Adventure Center, P.O. Box 1168, Oak Hill, WV 25901; (304) 469–2651 or (888) ACE–RAFT.

Contact: Superintendent, National Park Service, New River Gorge National River, P.O. Box 246, Glen Jean, WV 25846; (304) 465–0508.

• • • • • • • • • • • • • • • • • • • •

This woodsy rail-trail from Thurmond to Minden is one of the most popular among the New River Gorge's trails. In just a short distance you get fine views of the New River Gorge, an overview of one of the nation's most important historic railroad towns, and plenty of luscious hardwood forest that is home to white-tailed deer, raccoons, even black bears. It's ideal for families with young children, and yet can be worked into something more challenging using the gorge's network of interlinking trails.

The trail dates back to the early 1900s, when it was constructed as the Arbuckle Branch of the Chesapeake & Ohio Railroad to haul coal from the mines of Minden to mainline trains in the boomtown of Thurmond, located just across the river. After the Arbuckle Branch was abandoned in the 1970s, it was converted into a trail thanks to the efforts of a local hiking club. The National Park Service got into the act in 1978, when it began managing the New River Gorge National River. It's therefore extremely well maintained and well marked.

From the Thurmond trailhead go around the gate, passing the trail's only portable toilet. Right away you meet up with the riffling Dunloup Creek. The grade is gentle at first, but you definitely soon notice a bit of a climb. In less than half a mile you come to the junction with the Dunloup Creek Trail, to the right (no bikes), which connects with the Southside-Brooklyn Trail (see Trail 28). Go left, uphill, into a peaceful realm of poplar, maple, and oak, mixed with pawpaw, redbud, and hydrangea. The New River's distant roar tangles with the cheery twitters of songbirds flitting all about.

You pass by one of the old railroad cairns, and, about a mile from the trailhead, come to the first—and longest—of the trail's five bridges.

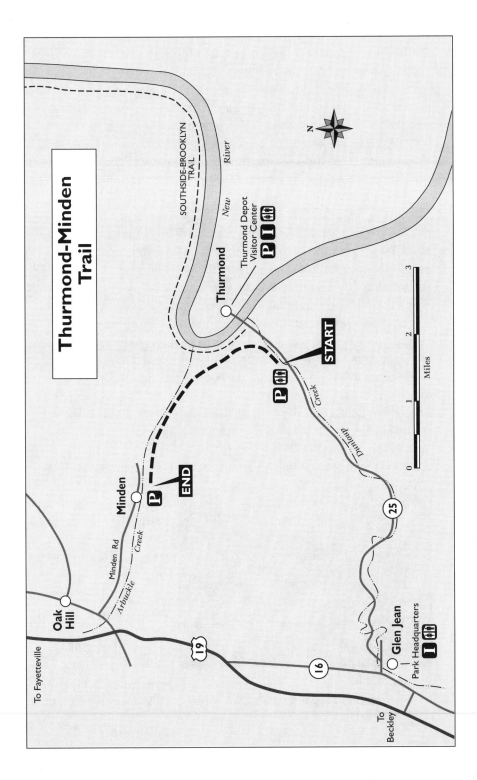

Farther along are two overlooks of the old railroad town of Thurmond, across the New River. Tons of coal from area mines were loaded up on the C&O Railway there, making Thurmond one of the richest towns anywhere along the railroad. Indeed, its streets bustled for the first twenty years of the twentieth century, its stores, saloons, hotels, and boardinghouses constantly overflowing. Today the town is a preserved time capsule of the railroad's golden age, with the old depot restored as a visitor center and little museum.

Onward, railroad ties scatter beside the trail, ever constant reminders of the corridor's past. At mile 1.3 you come to a huge boulder blocking the trail; apparently it's been here awhile, and some say it even contributed to the rail line's abandonment. Enjoy the great views of Thurmond from here, then climb up and around on the wooden staircase (not so easy with a bike).

At the overlook just before the second bridge, you are treated to gorgeous views of the New River cradled among tree-cloaked mountains—the essence of West Virginia beauty. Look carefully for coal-laden trains chugging along the gorge, though the coal these days comes from outside the gorge. In summer, the tiny white dots are white-water rafts floating down the river, which is considered one of the East's premier rafting rides. Just beyond you come to the Arbuckle Creek connector on the right, another link with the Southside-Brooklyn Trail.

Leaving the New behind, the trail soon follows Arbuckle Creek, a

pretty stream coursing deep in the ravine to the right. You cross over another trestle, then pass through an especially prolific section of rhododendrons, which burst into a frenzy of pastel blooms in early July. Cross over the trail's fourth bridge, this one curved, then

A biker on the Thurmond-Minden Trail spots the former boomtown of Thurmond across the New River.

The magnificent New River and the tree-cloaked Allegheny Mountains can be seen from an overlook along the Thurmond-Minden Trail.

pass another cement cairn. Soon you cross the fifth trestle, signaling your final descent to Minden, and a splashing waterfall appears on the right. Near the top of the trail, watch for the whistlepost with a W on it; it once alerted the engineer to blow his whistle to announce the train's arrival.

The trail ends at a gate, depositing you amid small houses. Turn around and enjoy it all again, this time with a downhill advantage.

30 West Fork River Trail

Meandering along the placid West Fork River, this popular local trail passes by farmland and river bluffs, residential and commercial areas.

Activities:

Notes: Biking this trail requires a mountain bike or hybrid.

Location: Between Fairmont and Shinnston in Harrison and Marion Counties

Length: 14.5 miles plus 1-mile spur; one-way

Surface: Packed limestone

Wheelchair access: Yes

Difficulty: Easy. The wide and level trail is easy to negotiate.

Food: Shinnston and Fairmont have groceries and restaurants.

Rest rooms: Worthington Park (mile 5.25) and Mary Lou Retton Youth Park (mile 15) have rest rooms.

Seasons: Open year-round.

Access and parking: There are a number of access points to this trail:

- *Shinnston* (southern terminus): From the Shinnston/Saltwell Road exit off I–79, turn left (west) and proceed 0.25 mile to the Exxon station. Turn left on Saltwell Road (WV–131) and follow this about 7 miles to U.S. 19 in Shinnston (traffic light). Turn right on U.S. 19 and go six blocks; turn left at St. Ann's Catholic Church, before the bridge across the West Fork River. Go 1 block and park along the city street. The trail begins under the U.S. 19 bridge. Future plans call for a trailhead parking lot to be built along U.S. 19.

- *Enterprise* (mile 3): From the Shinnston/Saltwell Road exit off I–79, turn left (west) and proceed 0.25 mile to the Exxon station, turning left on Saltwell Road (WV–131). Follow Saltwell Road about 7 miles to U.S. 19 in Shinnston (traffic light). Turn right onto U.S. 19, and proceed north about 2 miles to Enterprise. In Enterprise, watch for the bridge back across the West Fork River. At the end of the bridge, turn right and park beneath the bridge. Facing the river, the trail goes right (north) to Fairmont.

- *Worthington* (mile 5.25): From the Shinnston/Saltwell Road exit off I–79, turn left (west) and proceed 0.25 mile to the Exxon station. Turn left on Saltwell Road (WV–131) and go about 7 miles to U.S. 19 in Shinnston

 WEST VIRGINIA

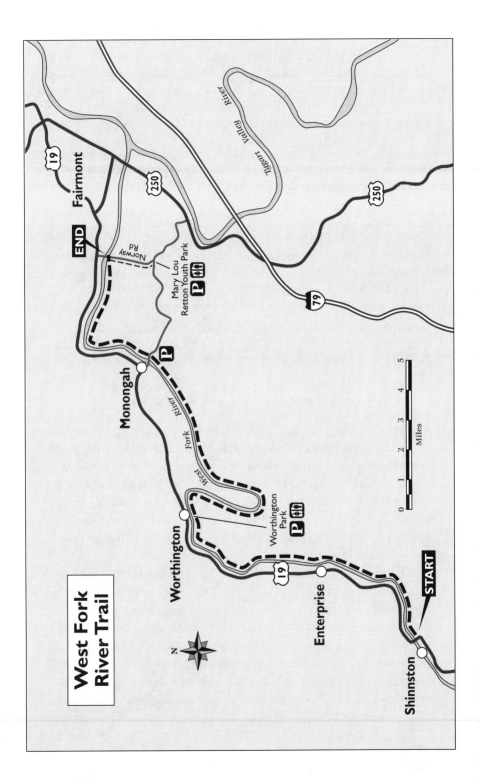

West Fork River Trail

(traffic light). Turn right onto U.S. 19 and proceed north about 5 miles to Worthington. Watch for the turn back (east) across the West Fork River. At the end of the bridge, turn right into Worthington Park. The trail is at the top of the park entrance. Cross the road to enter the trail north to Fairmont.

- *Monongah* (mile 10): From the Shinnston/Saltwell Road exit off I–79, turn left (west) and proceed 0.25 mile to the Exxon station. Turn left on Saltwell Road (WV–131) and go about 7 miles to U.S. 19 in Shinnston (traffic light). Turn right and proceed north on U.S. 19 about 7 miles to Monongah. Turn right at the Monongah Middle School, then left at the stop sign. There is a large parking lot adjoining the trail.

- *Fairmont* (northern terminus): From the U.S. 250 exit (exit 132) off I–79, go north on U.S. 250. At the Pizza Hut turn left and follow Mary Lou Retton Drive to Mary Lou Retton Youth Park. Park here, go to the top of the driveway, and follow signs approximately 1 mile on Norway Road to the trail. At the trail, turn left to go in the direction of Shinnston.

Rentals: No

Contact: Marion County Parks and Recreation Commission, P.O. Box 1258-316, Monroe Street, Fairmont, WV 26554; (304) 363–7037. North Harrison Rails to Trails Association, 35 Walnut Street, Shinnston, WV 26431; (304) 592–0177.

• • • • • • • • • • • • • • • • • • • •

Winding along the West Fork River in the rural heart of West Virginia, the West Fork River Trail connects a collection of small communities, each one boasting tail-wagging dogs and softball diamonds dotted with young players. Locals are the trail's primary users: lines of families on bikes, couples out for an evening stroll, young friends sauntering to a neighbor's house. For out-of-towners, the trail offers a glimpse into classic Americana, a spot that bigger places seem to have forgotten.

The coming of the Baltimore & Ohio Railroad in 1852 signaled the beginning of an industrial era for Marion County. Commercial shipments of coal developed into a major industry by the 1890s; the discovery of oil and gas in the Mannington area around the same time caused the population to explode. All this industrial prowess declined in the twentieth century, however, and railroad use waned. Eventually the corridor was abandoned. Active volunteers have since worked diligently to develop this well-fashioned rail-trail, with future plans to link it with the American Discovery Trail near Clarksburg and the Mon River Trail in Fairmont.

This narrative begins at the trail's southern trailhead in downtown Shinnston, beneath the U.S. 19 bridge, and follows the order of the mile markers north. Taking off along the West Fork River (really the West Fork Monongahela River, but never called that), you'll notice right away how the trail's limestone surface crunches noisily beneath your feet or bike tires. Benches dot the trailside every now and again, beckoning you to listen quietly for the breeze rustling through the treetops, Canada Geese making a splashdown, and water lapping upon the shore.

Around mile 2 you pass pretty peach-hued cliffs, with small white houses speckling the opposite shore. Honeysuckle perfumes the air, and in springtime redbud and dogwood add splashes of brightness to the new green woods.

At mile 3 you cut between the tidy little houses of Enterprise, where T-shirted men mow lawns, women hang colorful laundry, kids play tag. Cross County Road 19/2, and once again enter a hilly, woodsy scene. In another mile, a sign indicates you're leaving Har-

rison County for Marion County; just ahead, look on the left for the old, rusted railroad bridge spanning the river. Houses announce your arrival to the community of Hutchinson around mile 5. You pass by another baseball diamond and an old, burnt-out brick building, then amble among the now-familiar wooded hills. Just after passing a sewage treatment plant, you enter the town of Worthington (mile 5.25), where a waterfront park has swings and a softball field, and anglers stand waist-deep in the river's green waters below an old mill dam. Worthington is one of the bigger

This biker rides by one of the miniature waterfalls along the West Fork River Trail.

towns along the trail, but with only 233 souls, that's not saying much.

A really pretty section awaits just ahead; cut through sunny green slopes, then wrap around wooded hills laced with miniature waterfalls. Cross a railroad bridge over a little stream just beyond mile 8, then come to the town of Everson. Cross County Road 27, pass by a scattering of houses, and reenter the woods-and-river landscape.

Around mile 10 you cut across a dirt road then come to the town of Monongah. Cross a railroad trestle, then County Road 56. Pay close attention here, following the trail up and to the right, past an industrial yard and a baseball field. The scenery turns pastoral again, all the way to the town of Norway at mile 14. You can continue half a mile farther on the trail to a bridge spur and overlook or, if you go around the gate to the right, you can reach Mary Lou Retton Youth Park (named for the 1984 Olympic gold medalist from Marion County) about a mile away. To reach the park, turn left on the paved road (unmarked County Road 56/6), then take a quick right on the uphill road (unmarked Norway Road), through the little town of Norway. After a bit of an uphill climb, the park will be on your left, offering three baseball fields, a picnic area, tennis courts, a playground, and the West Virginia Miner's Memorial, along with parking and rest rooms.

While in the area, be sure to check out the McTrail (see "More Rail-Trails" at the end of this section of the book), which begins on Morgantown Avenue in Fairmont and takes you to Pricketts Fort State Park.

The West Fork River Trail is wide and level, making it easy to negotiate.

31   West Fork Trail

This isolated woodland trail visits small farms and remote mountain forests along the West Fork Greenbrier River. Great swimming and fishing may be enjoyed along its entire length.

Activities:

Notes: There is camping on National Forest lands. The 15 miles between Wildell and Durbin feature river rapids popular with canoeists and kayakers. Most of the trestles are not decked and still have open ties; horseback riders will have to detour through the streams.

Location: Between Greenbrier Junction and Durbin in Monongahela National Forest, in Pocahontas and Randolph Counties

Length: 25.5 miles one-way

Surface: Original ballast of crushed rock and cinders

Wheelchair access: Durbin provides access. Other points should be used at the discretion of the user, since slopes between Forest Road 44 and the trail vary.

Difficulty: Moderate. The fairly level slope and wide corridor are ideal for mountain biking, although bikers may experience minor problems in pockets where the dirt is not compacted.

Food: Facilities are few and far between. Glady has a small grocery store; there are groceries and a few small restaurants in Durbin.

Rest rooms: No public rest rooms available.

Seasons: Open year-round, with May through December seeing the most use. Autumn foliage is spectacular. Heavy snow may make long winter hikes difficult, but great for cross-country skiing.

Access and parking: The trail is accessible at the northernmost and southernmost points, and along Forest Road 44:

* *Glady:* The northernmost access point is in Glady. To reach Glady from Elkins, take U.S. 33 east from Elkins to Alpena. Turn south on County Road 27, located across from historic Alpine Lodge, and travel about 9 miles to Glady. The trailhead is located in the center of town. Park at the end of the road past the post office/grocery (not marked or signed as of publication date). From here you'll have to hike or bike to reach the trail's isolated terminus at Greenbrier Junction, or follow the trail south from Glady to Durbin.

- *Durbin:* The southern terminus is in Durbin, at the junction of U.S. 250 and County Road 250/15, east of the U.S. 250 bridge over the West Fork Greenbrier.
- *Forest Road 44:* There is access along Forest Road 44, which more or less parallels the trail, with several turnouts large enough for one or two cars.

Rentals: No

Contact: Monongahela National Forest, Greenbrier District, P.O. Box 67, Bartow, WV 24920, (304) 450-3335.

In late spring, bright pink and white rhododendron blossoms bedeck the West Fork Trail, lending a dainty touch to one of West Virginia's most wild and remote rail-trails. Crossing eight trestles, you meander beneath mixed hardwoods, hemlock, spruce, and pine along four different rivers, and explore the mountainous domain of beavers and black bears, white-tailed deer and foxes. There are few facilities along the way; it's just you and nature, and some of the best fishing holes around.

The rail bed was built by the Coal and Iron Railway Company between Elkins and Durbin in the early 1900s to haul lumber out of the Cheat Mountain area and upper Greenbrier River Valley. In 1905 it was sold to the Western Maryland Railway Company. After the timber industry declined in the 1920s, the railway began hauling coal from Cheat Mountain and Point Mountain coal fields. After the section between Greenbrier Junction and Durbin became obsolete, the Trust for Public Lands purchased the corridor, which then sold it to the U.S. Forest Service in 1986. The rail-trail plans have progressed ever since. Keep in mind that this trail is extremely rugged and isolated; no markers help keep track of mileage along the way.

The trail's shape is a bit of an oddity. Picture it as an upside-down fishhook, with the long shank running along the south-flowing West Fork Greenbrier River. The trail's northern terminus is at the hook's curved end, at isolated Greenbrier Junction—about 4 miles southwest of Glady—which you can't reach by car. Instead, you'll have to park at Glady, the trail's northernmost point, and proceed by bike or foot. Of course, this means you'll have to trudge along the most difficult (albeit quite scenic) part of the trail, only to backtrack to

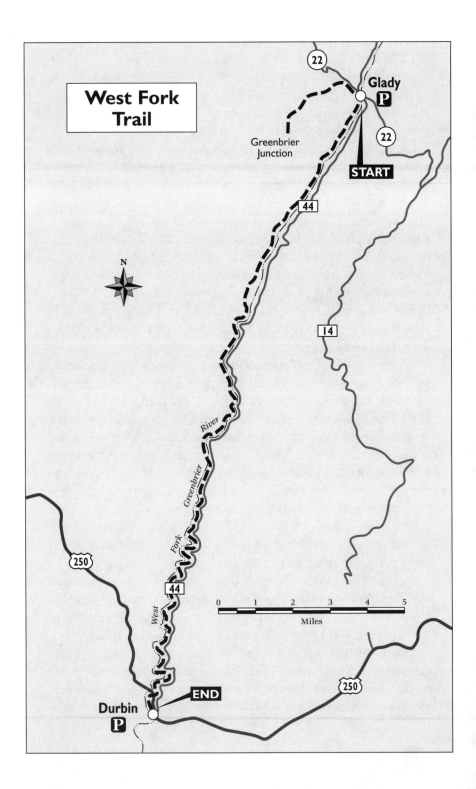

West Fork
Trail

Greenbrier
Junction

22

Glady
P

START

22

44

N

14

River

Greenbrier

Fork

250

44

West

0   1   2   3   4   5
Miles

END

250

Durbin
P

Glady before heading south along its long shank.

Regardless of whether you go to Greenbrier Junction or head immediately south, you should begin in Glady. Glady is tiny. The only thing here is the Glady Store, which has served as a post office since 1886 and now also sells food, soft drinks, candy, and other trail necessities. You'll find the trailhead near the center of the town; park on the street.

To reach Greenbrier Junction, head west on the trail. The journey from Glady to Greenbrier Junction offers some truly spectacular scenery as you voyage through forests of ash, maple, hemlock, and cherry along the lovely Shavers Fork. Bikers, however, may find some difficulties due to washed-out areas and fallen rock. About a quarter mile from town awaits wet and crumbling Tunnel #2, which should be bypassed (the Forest Service has blocked the entrance to dissuade trail users from entering). The best tactic is to ascend north to County Road 22, turn left, and rejoin the trail on the tunnel's west side.

In less than 2 miles you pass Cheat Junction, where the former railroad divided. Several primitive campsites are located in the surrounding forest lands. The trail fizzles about 1 mile farther at isolated Greenbrier Junction, perched on the banks of Shavers Fork.

From Greenbrier Junction, some people enjoy hiking on down to the High Falls of Cheat Trail, which connects with the West Fork Trail south of Glady. Otherwise, backtrack to Glady (sorry about the steep grade to Cheat Mountain) and head south, along the main segment of the trail. The trail surface south of Glady is really soft; even fat-tire bikes can mire down in the loose cinders. Passing through bucolic pasturelands dotted with sheep and cows, you soon spot a small graveyard (mile 4.1) on the left.

At mile 7.3 (3.5 miles south of Glady), watch for the intersection with the other end of the High Falls of Cheat Trail, marked with yellow blazes and heading up the mountain. Two miles farther down, the West Fork Trail crosses the north/south watershed of Glady Fork and the Greenbrier River. Where the hillsides nip together, Lynn Divide forms. At this point, rain flowing to the north of the divide heads for the Cheat River and on to Pittsburgh and the Ohio River. Meanwhile, rain falling to the south flows to the Greenbrier River, then to

Charleston and the Atlantic via the New and Kanawha Rivers.

The West Fork Greenbrier, which gives this trail its name, widens the farther south you go, its cattail-fringed banks blooming crazily with spring and summer wildflowers. Trestles whisk you back and forth across the river at miles 13.5, 13.7, 16.5 near the confluence with Iron Bridge Run, 18.7 at the confluence with Little River, and 23.9 at the Mountain Lick Run confluence. Between the trestles are great river views, fishing pools, wildflower-splashed meadows, and lovely rock formations.

Some 22 miles south of Glady you pass beneath the U.S. 250 bridge, thereby reaching the trail's southern terminus at a parking area off Pocahontas Road in Durbin. Approaching Durbin, bikers will love the two narrow, hard-packed lanes, apparently compacted by a trout-stocking truck that travels this way. Durbin boasts an absolutely charming depot that has been converted into the community center, with parking available.

Fifteen miles south of Durbin, this same rail corridor has been converted into the Greenbrier River Trail (see Trail 24); the West Virginia Rails-to-Trails Council has recently reached an agreement with the right-of-way's owner to grant access to a four-foot-wide trail that parallels this section of track. By the turn of the century, there should be an uninterrupted trail for 120 miles from North Caldwell to Glady. The Greenbrier River Trail and the West Fork Trail will then be part of the second longest trail in the country.

Wandering beside the riffling, boulder-strewn Williams River, this intimate rail-trail explores the gentler side of West Virginia's magnificently rugged mountains.

Activities:

Notes: Camping from March 15 to December 15 only. Paddlesports include canoeing.

Location: Tea Creek Recreation Area in Monongahela National Forest, Pocahontas County

Length: 2.2 miles one-way

Surface: Natural

Wheelchair access: No

Difficulty: Easy to moderate. The fairly flat riverside trail is easy for hikers; roots and ruts make it moderately difficult for bikers.

Food: Pack in your own. The nearest groceries and restaurants are in Marlinton. Elk River Touring Center, 8.8 miles north of the U.S. 219 junction with WV–150 in the community of Slatyfork, has a restaurant and lodging.

Rest rooms: There are vault toilets at Tea Creek Campground.

Seasons: Open year-round. Snowfall often closes WV–150, mid-December to mid-March, and roads are not plowed (some people ski in). Tea Creek Campground is open mid-March to mid-December, weather permitting.

Access and parking: From Marlinton, go north on U.S. 219 to WV–150 (Highland Scenic Highway) and turn west (left). In 8.9 miles take Forest Road 86 west (left) for a mile or so to the Tea Creek Campground exit on the right. Go over the cement bridge; the trailhead is marked at the right side of the parking area.

Rentals: Elk River Touring Center, U.S. 219, Slatyfork, WV 26291; (304) 572–3771. Located 8.8 miles north of U.S. 219 junction with WV–150, in community of Slatyfork; rents skis and bikes, and offers cross-country skiing and fly-fishing trips.

Contact: Assistant Ranger, Marlinton Ranger District, Tea Creek Recreation Area, P.O. Box 210, Marlinton, WV 24954-0210; (304) 799–4334.

• • • • • • • • • • • • • • • • • • •

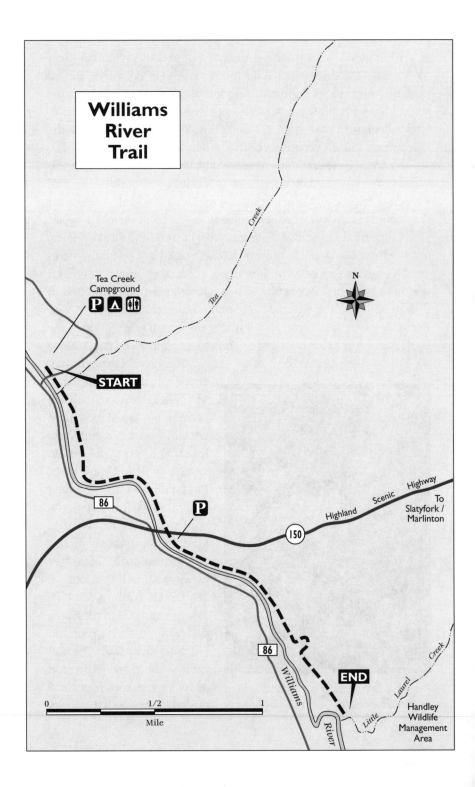

W hat glorious mountain country embraces the Williams River Trail. The drive to reach the trailhead, with its rank upon rugged rank of violet ridges fading off into the distance, is itself worth the trek. The Williams River Trail shows a gentler side to all this wildness, offering an easy stroll through pretty woodlands, alongside the cascading, trout-filled waters of the Williams River.

You are in the heart of the Tea Creek Recreation Area, a vast backcountry distinguished by steep mountain slopes, icy mountain creeks, luxuriant forests, and green fringed rock crops. Trails that crisscross the mountains here follow old rail beds dating from the early 1900s, when loggers stripped the mountainsides of trees and shipped them away via standard-gauge railway. These trails have become one of West Virginia's primo mountain-biking spots; they aren't so bad for hiking or cross-country skiing either. (Other area trails described in this guide include the Gauley Mountain Trail, see Trail 21; the Bear Pen Ridge Trail, see "More Rail-Trails" at the end of this section of the book; and the Tea Creek Mountain Trail, also under "More Rail-Trails.")

The Williams River Trail begins at the Tea Creek Campground.

A runner strides through a wooded thicket on the Williams River Trail.

Once an old logging camp with church and school, the site now offers rest rooms and portable water to transient hikers and bikers (as well as a place to spend the night). Find the trail across the footbridge above Tea Creek, its banks laced with Canada lilies. Proceed straight ahead, past the trailheads for the Tea Creek Mountain Trail and the Tea Creek Trail on the left. Just beyond, a sign reassures that you are, indeed, on the Williams River Trail. The trail itself is single-track dirt, full of rocks and tree roots and tiny creek crossings that make

The rock-strewn Williams River is fast-flowing and filled with trout.

it a rather technical bike ride; a walk or run is definitely easier. Pretty wildflowers bedeck the trailside, with the stars of the show being the rhododendrons. Off to the right, the river cascades over rocks and flows over large, smooth slabs of stone.

The river disappears for a brief spell, then reappears at your feet, with a steep, timbered ridge of Tea Creek Mountain rising on the left—very pretty. Watch for good spots to dip your toes. About a mile from the trailhead you pass beneath WV–150; wave to the people at the observation platform across the river. Just beyond, a spur trail on the left leads to a parking area and access to WV–150.

Farther along, ford a couple of tiny streams. Soon the trail detours away from the river into piney woods, and everything becomes quiet, save for the padding of your footsteps on soft pine needles. You cross a stream on a wooden bridge and wind through the woods some more, until the trail comes to an abrupt end at Little Laurel Creek, just above where it meets the Williams River. Silvery and mirror smooth, the creek meanders through a pretty meadow here dotted with bursts of purple and yellow wildflowers and shouldered by wooded mountains. Ahead, across the creek, lies the Handley Wildlife Management Area, good for more hiking but no bikes allowed. If you are able to ford the stream, you can continue for 0.8 mile to Williams River Road.

MORE RAIL-TRAILS

Bear Pen Ridge Trail

Located in the popular Tea Creek Recreation Area, this trail is unique from the others in the area in that it features Pottsville sandstone dotted with young spruce. Accessed from the Gauley Mountain Trail or Tea Creek Trail, its eastern portion travels along an old railroad grade, while the western section uses an old road on steep terrain. (Other trails in the Tea Creek area described in this guide are the Gauley Mountain Trail, see Trail 21; the Williams River Trail, see Trail 32; and the Tea Creek Mountain Trail, located here under "More Rail-Trails.")

Activities: 🥾 ⛏ 🚲 ⛷ 🏂

Location: Tea Creek Recreation Area in Monongahela National Forest, Pocahontas County

Length: 3.5 miles one-way

Surface: Natural

Wheelchair access: No

Difficulty: Moderate

Food: Pack in your own. The nearest groceries and restaurants are in Marlinton. Also, Elk River Touring Center, 8.8 miles north of the U.S. 219 junction with WV–150 in the community of Slatyfork, has a restaurant (plus lodging).

Rest rooms: No

Seasons: Open year-round. Snowfall often closes WV–150 mid-December to mid-March, and Tea Creek Campground is closed mid-December to mid-March.

Access and parking: The trail is in the middle of the Tea Creek Recreation Area network of trails, north of Marlinton. Access it off of the Gauley Mountain Trail (see Trail 21) or the Tea Creek Trail, 4.5 miles east of Tea Creek Campground on the Williams River Trail (see Trail 32).

Rentals: Elk River Touring Center, U.S. 219, Slatyfork, WV 26291; (304) 572–3771; located 8.8 miles north of U.S. 219 junction with WV–150, in the community of Slatyfork; rents skis and bikes, and offers cross-country skiing and fly-fishing trips.

Contact: Assistant Ranger, Marlinton Ranger District, Tea Creek Recreation Area, P.O. Box 210, Marlinton, WV 24954–0210; (304) 799–4334.

Clover Trail

This short pathway follows the route of an old railroad grade where, in the process of winding up the mountain, the train would roll along one switchback, then go backward on the next. It connects Clover Run Road and the 3.6-mile Pheasant Mountain Trail.

Activities:

Location: Pheasant Mountain Area in Monongahela National Forest, Tucker County

Length: 2 miles one-way

Surface: Natural

Wheelchair access: No

Difficulty: Moderate

Food: No

Rest rooms: No

Seasons: Open year-round.

Access and parking: From Parsons, drive 0.4 mile north on WV–72 to Mount Zion Road (County Road 17). Turn left and proceed to County Road 21; turn left again to the trailhead, on the left.

Rentals: No

Contact: Cheat Ranger District, Monongahela National Forest, P.O. Box 368, Parsons, WV 26287; (304) 478–3251.

Elk River Trail

The state's only rail with trail, built along an inactive Conrail line, this trail follows the Elk River. Its future is up in the air; it may remain a short demonstration project or be extended 40 miles or more along the inactive tracks.

Activities:

Notes: Mountain bikes and hybrid bikes can be used on this trail.

Location: Between Kanawha County's Coonskin Park and downtown Charleston

Length: 1 mile one-way

Surface: Gravel

Wheelchair access: No

Difficulty: Easy

Food: Charleston has groceries and restaurants.

Rest rooms: At Coonskin Park

Seasons: Open year-round.

Access and parking: Since the southern trailhead does not have much parking, it's recommended to begin at the northern trailhead at Coonskin Park, north of downtown Charleston. Take WV 114 north about 5 miles to Coonskin Drive. To find the southern trailhead from downtown Charleston, pass Fazio's Restaurant on Bullit Street, cross the railroad tracks, and turn left on Slack Street. Follow Slack north along the Elk River; the street name changes to Barlow Drive in about a mile. Barlow ends at the southern trailhead.

Rentals: Ridge Rider Mountain Bikers, 405 Capitol Street, Charleston, WV 25301; (304) 343–7430.

Contact: Kanawha County Parks & Recreation, 200 Coonskin Drive, Charleston, WV 25301; (304) 341–8000. Elk River Rails to Trails Foundation, P.O. Box 555, Charleston, WV 25305.

Lumberjack Trail

Following an old railroad grade, this forested trail explores the north slope of Spruce Knob. Watch for the occasional cross ties and bridge footings that date from railroading days.

Activities:

Location: Spruce Knob Unit of Spruce Knob–Seneca Rocks National Recreation Area, Randolph and Pendleton Counties

Length: 3.3 miles one-way

Surface: Natural

Wheelchair access: No

Difficulty: Easy

Food: No

Rest rooms: No

Seasons: Open year-round.

Access and parking: In the Spruce Knob Unit of Spruce Knob–Seneca Rocks National Recreation Area, you'll find the southern trailhead just south of a prominent switchback on Forest Road 112 (4.5 miles from Spruce Knob Lake). Parking is possible along Forest Road 112.

Rentals: No

Contact: Potomac Ranger District, HC 59, Box 240, Petersburg, WV 26847; (304) 257–4488.

McTrail (Marion County Trail)

Running beside Pricketts Creek through rural Marion County, this short trail features a 1,200-foot lighted tunnel and, at its northern end, Pricketts Fort State Park, a reconstruction of a refuge fort built on the Virginia frontier in 1774.

Activities:

Notes: Mountain bikes and hybrid bikes can be used on this trail.

Location: Northeast Fairmont to Pricketts Fort State Park, in Marion County

Length: 2.5 miles one-way

Surface: Packed cinders and gravel

Wheelchair access: Yes

Difficulty: Easy

Food: Fairmont has restaurants and groceries.

Rest rooms: At Pricketts Fort

Seasons: Open year-round.

Access and parking: The northern trailhead is at Pricketts Fort State Park. The southern trailhead is located behind Mountain State Metals on Morgantown Avenue in northeast Fairmont.

Rentals: Whitetail Bicycles, 219 Jefferson Street, Fairmont, WV 26554; (304) 366–0439.

Contact: Marion County Parks and Recreation Commission, P.O. Box 1258-316, Monroe Street, Fairmont, WV 26554; (304) 363–7037.

Moore Run Trail

This surprisingly gentle, slow climb up McGowan Mountain in the wild Otter Creek Wilderness plays cat and mouse with cascade-rippled Moore Run. Among its features are high-altitude bogs similar to those at Cranberry Glades in the Gauley Ranger District and at Dolly Sods on the Allegheny Front. (Also in the Otter Creek Wilderness is the popular Otter Creek Trail, see "More Rail-Trails" later in this section.)

Activities:

Location: Otter Creek Wilderness in Monongahela National Forest, Randolph County

Length: 4.1 miles one-way

Surface: Natural

Wheelchair access: No

Difficulty: Difficult. This is rugged territory, where trails are neither signed nor blazed, deadfall trees are not cleared unless they create an environmental impact, and there are no bridges at creek crossings.

Food: Nothing along the trail. Elkins and Parsons, the nearest cities, have restaurants and groceries.

Rest rooms: No

Seasons: Closed mid-April to mid-August to allow wild turkey and black bear to rear their young.

Access and parking: You can access the trail off the Otter Creek Trail (see "More Rail-Trails" later in this section) or the McGowan Mountain Trail.

Rentals: No

Contact: Cheat Ranger District, Monongahela National Forest, P.O. Box 368, Parsons, WV 26287; (304) 478–3251.

Narrow Gauge Trail

This portion of an old 8.5-mile right-of-way descends down Mann's Creek to one of the area's old coke mines.

Activities:

Location: Babcock State Park, in Fayette County

Length: 2.4 miles

Surface: Crushed stone and dirt

Wheelchair access: No

Difficulty: Moderate

Food: Babcock State Park has a restaurant.

Rest rooms: At Babcock State Park

Seasons: Open year-round.

Access and parking: The northern trailhead is on the west side of the park road, between the north cabin area and campground. The southern trailhead is 1.5 miles down Old Sewell Road from the gristmill and park office.

Rentals: No

Contact: Babcock State Park, HC 35, Box 150, Clifftop, WV 25831-9801; (304) 438–3004.

Otter Creek Trail

Lying in a bowl shaped by Shavers and McGowan Mountains, the gorgeous Otter Creek Wilderness is rapidly becoming a popular backcountry destination for Washingtonians. Once crisscrossed with tracks laid by the Otter Creek Boom and Lumber Company, the area's trees have since grown back, forming a wonderful mixed hardwoods canopy filled with white-tailed deer and black bear, snowshoe hare and wild turkey. The most popular trail is the Otter Creek Trail, which features waterfalls, limestone springs, deep swimming holes, and the constant companionship of cascading Otter Creek—a truly spectacular hike. (Also in the Otter Creek Wilderness is the Moore Run Trail, see "More Rail-Trails" earlier in this section.)

Activities:

Location: Otter Creek Wilderness, in the Cheat Ranger District of Monongahela National Forest, Tucker County

Length: 11.4 miles one-way

Surface: Natural

Wheelchair access: No

Difficulty: Difficult. This is rugged territory, where trails are neither signed nor blazed, deadfall trees are not cleared unless they create an environmental impact, and there are no bridges at creek crossings.

Food: Nothing along the trail. Elkins and Parsons, the nearest cities, have restaurants and groceries.

Rest rooms: No

Seasons: Open year-round. The trail crosses Otter Creek three times, which is no problem in midsummer or fall, but heavy spring floods can make the stream impossible to cross. Spring and heavy rains make it nearly impossible not to get your feet wet.

Access and parking: Take WV–72 east of Parsons; 2 miles south of Hendricks is a parking area for twenty vehicles and the trailhead for the Otter Creek Trail.

Rentals: No

Contact: Cheat Ranger District, Monongahela National Forest, P.O. Box 368, Parsons, WV 26287; (304) 478–3251.

Railroad Grade Trail

Following an old logging railroad grade through pretty deciduous forest in the Canaan Mountain area, this trail still turns up old ties harking back to its railroading days.

Activities:

Location: Cheat Ranger District in Monongahela National Forest, Tucker County

Length: 3.1 miles one-way

Surface: Natural

Wheelchair access: No

Difficulty: Moderate

Food: No

Rest rooms: No

Seasons: Open year-round. From late December to mid-March, snow turns this trail into an idyllic cross-country ski path. Likewise, snow may close the Canaan Loop Trail Road, preventing northern access to this trail.

Access and parking: In Blackwater Falls State Park, proceed east past the lodge on the park road, which becomes the Canaan Loop Road (Forest Road 13). One mile beyond the Lindy Run trailhead, you'll see the northern trailhead for the Railroad Grade Trail. If you continue on the loop road, you'll come around to the trail's southern trailhead.

Rentals: Blackwater Bikes, William Avenue, Davis, WV 26260; (304) 259–5286. Blackwater Falls State Park (304–259–5216) also rents bikes.

Contact: Cheat Ranger District, US Forest Service, P.O. Box 368, Parsons, WV 26282; (304) 478–3251.

Red Creek Trail

Designated in 1975 as a place for natural forces to take their course, Dolly Sods Wilderness is absolutely stunning with its windswept plateaus, upland bogs, beaver ponds, and sweeping vistas. The longest and most heavily used trail is the Red Creek Trail, an old railroad grade that follows rippling Red Creek.

Activities:

Location: Dolly Sods Wilderness in Monongahela National Forest, Tucker County

Length: 3 miles one-way

Surface: Natural

Wheelchair access: No

Difficulty: Difficult. Be prepared for primitive conditions; the trail is not maintained for the casual hiker. There are no markings or blazes, and no bridges at the two crossings over Red Creek. At high water times, hikers will have to alter their plans.

Food: No

Rest rooms: No

Seasons: Open year-round. Winter brings heavy snows, sometimes making access impossible.

Access and parking: From WV–32 south of Canaan Valley Resort State Park, go east on County Road 45 to Laneville (a small collection of cabins on Red Creek). Parking is available here.

Rentals: No

Contact: Monongahela National Forest, Box 1548, Elkins, WV 26241; (304) 636–1800.

Stone Camp Run Trail

Following portions of an old railroad grade up a deep hollow on Middle Mountain, this trail weaves back and forth across Stone Camp Run, through a pretty forest of beech, cherry, birch, and maple.

Activities:

Location: Laurel Fork Wilderness in Monongahela National Forest, Tucker County

Length: 1.5 miles one-way

Surface: Natural

Wheelchair access: No

Difficulty: Moderate

Food: No

Rest rooms: No

Seasons: Open year-round. Winter brings heavy snows, sometimes making access impossible.

Access and parking: From Wymer on U.S. 33/WV-55, go south 9.3 miles on Forest Road 14 to the signed trailhead. There is parking for six cars.

Rentals: No

Contact: Greenbrier Ranger District, Monongahela National Forest, Box 25, Bartow, WV 24920; (304) 456-3335.

Tea Creek Mountain Trail

A less traveled route in the popular Tea Creek Recreation Area, this sinewy, hilly trail winds up and over Tea Creek Mountain, featuring wonderful views of the Cranberry Wilderness. (Other trails in the Tea Creek area described in this guide are the Gauley Mountain Trail, see Trail 21; the Williams River Trail, see Trail 32; and the Bear Pen Ridge Trail, see earlier in this section under "More Rail-Trails.")

Activities:

Location: Tea Creek Recreation Area in Monongahela National Forest, Pocahontas County

Length: 7 miles one-way

Surface: Natural

Wheelchair access: No

Difficult: Difficult for bikes, moderate for hikers

Food: Pack in your own. The nearest groceries and restaurants are in Marlinton. Elk River Touring Center, 8.8 miles north of the U.S. 219 junction with WV-150 in the community of Slatyfork, has a restaurant (plus lodging).

Rest rooms: There are vault toilets at Tea Creek Campground.

Seasons: Open year-round. Snowfall often closes WV-150 mid-December to mid-March. Tea Creek Campground is closed mid-December to mid-March.

Access and parking: From Marlinton, go north on U.S. 219 to WV–150 (Highland Scenic Highway) and turn west (left). The trail's eastern access is directly across from the Little Laurel Overlook, near the south terminus of the Right Fork of Tea Creek Trail. The western access is farther down WV–150; take the Forest Road 86 west (left) exit and drive for a mile or so down the gravel road to the Tea Creek Campground, across the cement bridge. From the parking area here, follow the Williams Creek Trail across the bridge over Tea Creek, to the junction with the Williams River Trail and Tea Creek Trail.

Rentals: Elk River Touring Center, U.S. 219, Slatyfork, WV 26291; (304) 572–3771; located 8.8 miles north of the U.S. 219 junction with WV–150, in community of Slatyfork; rents skis and bikes, and offers cross-country skiing and fly-fishing trips.

Contact: Assistant Ranger, Marlinton Ranger District, Tea Creek Recreation Area, P.O. Box 210, Marlinton, WV 24954-0210; (304) 799-4334.

ABOUT THE AUTHOR

A California native, Barbara A. Noe moved to the Washington, D.C., area in 1993 for an internship with *National Geographic Traveler* and has lived there ever since. When she's not working as the Associate Travel Editor for National Geographic Books, she can be found hiking the Blue Ridge, training for marathons, or biking along the C&O Canal as well as in Europe and Canada.

Her travel pieces have appeared in the *Boston Globe,* the *Bangor Daily News, Reader's Digest,* and *National Geographic Traveler;* her *National Geographic Guide to 100 Easy Hikes in Northern Virginia, Maryland, Washington, D.C., and Delaware* is scheduled for publication in spring 2000.

FREE T!*

*with a $50 contribution or more

100% cotton T-shirt with Rails-to-Trails Conservancy logo printed on the front; and a circle of trail users printed in royal blue on back.

Join RAILS-TO-TRAILS CONSERVANCY NOW, get a FREE T-SHIRT and connect yourself with the largest national trail-building organization. As a member of Rails-to-Trails Conservancy, you will receive the following benefits:

- *Rails to Trails*, a colorful magazine dedicated to celebrating trails and greenways, published four times a year
- A free copy of *Sampler of America's Rail-Trails*
- Discounts on publications, merchandise and conferences
- A free t-shirt with your contribution of $50 or more
- Additional membership benefits for Trailblazer Society members, including invitation to the annual rail-trail excursions

Most importantly, you will have the satisfaction that comes from helping to build a nationwide network of beautiful trails for all of us to enjoy for years and generations to come.

PLEASE JOIN TODAY by calling toll-free: 1-800-888-7747, ext. 11 (credit card orders only), or mail your membership contribution with the form on the following page, or see our web site, **www.railtrails.org**.

RAILS-TO-TRAILS CONSERVANCY • *Connecting People and Communities*

RAILS to TRAILS CONSERVANCY

Yes! I want to join Rails-to-Trails Conservancy!

Send me my member packet, including my *Sampler of America's Rail-Trails,* one year (four issues) of *Rails to Trails,* the colorful magazine that celebrates trails and greenways and my FREE T-SHIRT with my contribution of $50 or more. I will also receive discounts on publications, merchandise and conferences. Here is my membership gift of:

❑ $18 – Individual
❑ $25 – Supporting
❑ $50 – Patron *(Free t-shirt at this giving level or higher!)*

T-shirt size XL only

❑ $100 – Benefactor
❑ $500 – Advocate
❑ $1,000 – Trailblazer Society
❑ Other $ _____

❑ Monthly Giving, *please see box below*

PAYMENT METHOD: ❑ VISA ❑ MasterCard ❑ American Express
Card # _____ Exp. Date _____
Signature _____

Member Name _____
Street _____
City _____ State _____ Zip _____
Telephone _____ email _____

Rails-to-Trails Conservancy is a non-profit charitable 501(c)(3) organization. Contributions are tax-deductible.

I want to support Rails-to-Trails Conservancy in the smartest, easiest and best way possible by donating monthly. Enclosed is my first monthly gift of:

❑ $5   ❑ $10   ❑ $15   ❑ Other $_____ *($5 minimum monthly contribution, please)*

Charge my future monthly gifts to my :

❑ Checking Account — Please transfer the amount indicated from my bank account each month
❑ Credit Card — Please charge the amount indicated to my credit card each month: ❑ VISA   ❑ MasterCard   ❑ American Express

Card Number: _____ Exp. Date: _____
Signature: _____ Date: _____

PAPERLESS PLEDGE AUTHORIZATION: I authorize Rails-to-Trails Conservancy to transfer my monthly contribution from my bank account or to charge my credit card (whichever I have indicated). I understand I may cancel or change my monthly pledge at any time by notifying Rails-to-Trails Conservancy. A record of each payment will appear on my monthly bank or credit card statement and will serve as my receipt.

Signature: _____ Date Signed: _____

EFT

Rails-to-Trails Conservancy
1100 17th St. NW • Washington, DC 20036
1-800-888-7747, ext. 11 (credit card orders only) • www.railtrails.org

To contact our membership department, please call (202) 974-5105 or email rtchelen@transact.org

RAILS to TRAILS CONSERVANCY